Television Westerns
1950 – 1980

Television Westerns
1950 – 1980

Lanny Tucker

Television Westerns 1950 – 1980

© Copyright 2022 by Lanny Tucker

All Rights Reserved.

No portion of this publication may be reproduced, stored, and/or copied electronically (except for academic use as a source), nor transmitted in any form or by any means without the prior written permission of the publisher and/or author.

Published in the United States of America by:

BearManor Media
1317 Edgewater Dr #110
Orlando FL 32804
bearmanormedia.com

Printed in the United States.

Ownership of the photographs within this book are neither claimed, nor implied, by the author.

Typesetting and layout by DataSmith Solutions

Cover by DataSmith Solutions

ISBN — 978-1-62933-838-5

Table of Contents

The Golden Age. 1

The Legends – *Gunsmoke* & *Bonanza* 2

Sixteen Shows Which Lasted Five Years or More 29

A Man Called Shenandoah to Zorro ~ ~
The Remainder of Television Westerns. 47

Reflections, Facts, & Opinions 111

Images of a Golden Time. 117

References 150

Index of shows 152

Index of actors 155

About the author 159

"Return with us now to those thrilling days of yesteryear!"

– *The Lone Ranger*

The Golden Age

The age of Television Westerns had its beginning in 1950 with programs aimed at children. By the middle of the decade, adult oriented shows had arrived. The genre peaked with the 1958–'59 season, remained immensely popular several more years, then started a decline.

Television Westerns attempts to examine programs – both children and adult – which aired from 1950 through 1980. With a couple of exceptions, the book is limited to prime-time programs.

To be included, a show had to be set during the approximately half century of the Old West. This leaves out frontier shows such as *Daniel Boone*, and contemporary programs like *Cowboy in Africa*.

Westerns with settings outside the continental United States are included.

In addition to a synopsis of each program and its cast members, efforts were made to include each show's best ratings, the show's creator, and the writer(s) of its theme song. Those lacking are because the information could not be found.

The television west's two greatest series, *Gunsmoke* and *Bonanza*, are examined in detail. Sixteen shows which lasted a minimum of five years are discussed at length, and the remaining programs are summarized.

A large majority of the lead actors are gone. For them, the year of their passing and their age at death are given.

The Legends –
Gunsmoke & Bonanza

Gunsmoke

1955 – 1975, CBS, 635 episodes: 233 thirty-minute black & white, 176 one-hour black & white, 226 one-hour color.

Cast:

James Arness as Matt Dillon
Milburn Stone as Galen "Doc" Adams
Amanda Blake as Kitty Russell, 1955-1974
Dennis Weaver as Chester Goode, 1955-1964
Ken Curtis as Festus Haggen, 1964-1975
Burt Reynolds as Quint Asper, 1962-1965
Glenn Strange as Sam the bartender, 1962-1974
Roger Ewing as Thad Greenwood, 1966-1967
Buck Taylor as Newly O'Brien, 1969-1975

Ratings:

Year	Rank
1955-56	Not available
1956-57	7th
1957-58	1st
1958-59	1st
1959-60	1st
1960-61	1st
1961-62	3rd
1962-63	10th
1963-64	20th
1964-65	27th
1965-66	30th
1966-67	34th
1967-68	4th
1968-69	6th
1969-70	2nd

1970-71	5th
1971-72	4th
1972-73	7th
1973-74	15th
1974-75	26th

This show was based upon the radio program of the same name, created by John Meston and Norman Macdonnell.

The theme song (also known as "Old Trails") was composed by Rex Koury and Glenn Spencer.

Made for Television Movies:
Gunsmoke – Return to Dodge 1987
Gunsmoke – The Last Apache 1990
Gunsmoke – To the Last Man 1992
Gunsmoke – The Long Ride 1993
Gunsmoke – One Man's Justice 1994

Synopsis:

When considering the dozens and dozens of shows in the Television West, one is regarded as best: *Gunsmoke*, starring James Arness as Matt Dillon.

Gunsmoke premiered on September 10, 1955. The program ran for twenty years as a weekly series, a record for a show with continuing characters which was later broken by *Law & Order: Special Victims Unit*. The show aired 635 episodes, a record which still stood in late 2021.

When cancelled in May, 1975 *Gunsmoke* was still a popular program, ranking 26th for the year. From 1987 through 1994, five *Gunsmoke* television movies were produced.

What made *Gunsmoke* so popular? How did it manage to successfully entertain millions during five decades of television episodes and movies? Why does the show continue to be watched on various channels, more than forty-five years after being cancelled?

Begin with the star, James Arness. Add Amanda Blake as Kitty Russell, Milburn Stone as Doc Adams, Dennis Weaver as Chester Goode, and Ken Curtis as Festus Haggen. Continue with writer John Meston, producers Norman Macdonnell and John Mantley, and a wealth of other talented writers, directors, and actors. And consider how the fictional Old West was portrayed at that time.

Before *Gunsmoke*, the Western as entertainment was considered to be children's fare. The heroes often wore white hats and shot to disarm, not kill. The outlaws usually wore black and were defeated – but not seriously hurt – most times.

This started to change in 1951, when writer John Meston and producer Norman Macdonnell approached CBS Radio with an idea for a weekly series, an adult Western called *Jeff Spain*.

The show was to be set in wild Dodge City, Kansas, in the days of buffalo hunters and cattle drives, about a United States marshal who shot to kill.

CBS said no, such a concept wouldn't have a chance.

But in early 1952, CBS Radio suddenly found themselves with a thirty-minute opening in their weekly schedule.

Executives remembered Meston and Macdonnell, and gave them the go-ahead on two conditions. The show's title had to be *Gunsmoke*, and the lead character could not be Jeff Spain, a name which sounded more outlaw than hero.

The name Mark Dillon was agreed upon. Meston, being a Western historian, said Mark was too modern a name. He recommended Matt, and CBS said fine.

On April 26, 1952, *Gunsmoke* had its radio premier. William Conrad, later to star in the television series *Cannon* and *Jake and the Fatman*, was the voice of Dillon. Parley Baer was Chester, Georgia Ellis played Miss Kitty, and Howard McNear, later to be Floyd the barber on *Andy Griffith*, was Doc Adams.

The first episode featured a youthful Billy the Kid committing two murders and escaping, with Matt Dillon gunning down a town bully inciting a mob. The audience loved it, and *Gunsmoke* was off on a nine-year run.

In 1955, CBS decided to add *Gunsmoke* to their expanding television lineup. Rather than take Macdonell away from his successful radio show, CBS hired Western film maker Charles Marquis Warren as producer. Warren later created and produced another successful Western, *Rawhide*.

Warren did not seriously consider *Gunsmoke's* radio stars for television. Although William Conrad had a perfect voice for the part, Warren thought his physical build would not be an imposing enough marshal.

Twenty-five actors auditioned for the role of Matt Dillon. Among those tested were Richard Boone (*Have Gun Will Travel*), Raymond Burr (*Perry Mason, Ironside*), and Denver Pyle (Uncle Jesse on *The Dukes of Hazard*).

The last man Warren looked at had been recommended by a friend, John Wayne. James Arness, all six feet, seven inches of him, turned out to be perfect.

Wayne, upon hearing the news, offered to introduce the first episode. Warren quickly agreed.

Viewers of the first episode, "Matt Gets It," were in for a shock. Dillon challenged a gunfighter and was shot down. The marshal recovered and went after the outlaw again. But this time, Dillon forced the action from farther away. The outlaw was again faster, but missed, and Dillon got him.

With that episode the foundation was laid for the first three-dimensional character in Western television. Marshal Matt Dillon, as developed by James Arness, was willing to risk his life for what he believed in. He was a fast draw, but there were others who were faster. He was a tough fighter, but there were others who were tougher. Dillon was usually successful. But not always.

Matt Dillon agonized over the decisions he had to make. He hated the taking of human life, but often had to.

Perhaps Dillon's outlook was best summarized in the following soliloquy, made as he walked among the graves on Boot Hill: "Out here I remind myself how violence ends. Some of these men are the victims of aimless slaughter. The rest I killed myself. The law comes hard to the frontier. Men like these didn't want it."

"And more men, still alive in Dodge City, don't want it. They have to be met. It's a chancy job. It makes a man watchful and a little lonely, but somebody has to do it." (From "Hack Prine," written by John Meston.)

Matt Dillon was not able to marry the woman he probably loved, Kitty Russell, because society of the time would not permit a lawman to marry a saloon girl. Such in-depth characterization was more than viewers of the 1950's were used to. But it was something they were ready for, and liked.

Arness, a decorated veteran of World War II, died in 2011 at the age of 88.

Gunsmoke forever changed the face of Western television. It ushered in the Adult Western, with numerous shows following. *Gunsmoke*, the first, outlasted them all.

Charles Marquis Warren kept the style and spirit of radio's *Gunsmoke* intact for television. The only major change was to make the character of Chester a cripple, giving him an excuse to always be lounging around the jail.

Actor Dennis Weaver was first turned down for the role of Chester Goode. When told a little humor was needed for the character, Weaver asked for a second chance. Adding his native Arkansas/Missouri drawl to the reading, Weaver won the part.

Chester wasn't a fighter. But he was loyal to a fault, always addressing the marshal as "Mister Dillon." Chester brewed a mean cup of coffee, loved to argue with Doc Adams, and could shoot with accuracy. In 1959, Weaver won an Emmy Award for his portrayal.

In the early 1960's Weaver decided he had taken the character of Chester Goode as far as he could, and began searching for his own show. He found it in 1964, and Chester limped into the sunset as Weaver starred in *Kentucky Jones* (which only lasted one season).

Weaver later starred for seven years in NBC's *McCloud*, as a modern Western lawman in New York.

Weaver died in 2006, at the age of 81.

With Weaver's departure the producers brought in Ken Curtis, a singing cowboy who had gained a small amount of fame in the 1940's, to play hillbilly deputy Festus Haggen.

Curtis had a more physical presence than Weaver, and Festus was handier with his fists and a gun than Chester. Curtis's abilities also broadened the show's ability to do comedy.

Festus referred to the marshal as "Matthew." Like Chester, Festus was sometimes perplexed by Doc Adams and loved to argue with him, often calling the doctor an "old scutter."

Curtis died in 1991, at the age of 72.

As Weaver was winding up his stint as Chester and Curtis was starting his run as Festus, future movie superstar Burt Reynolds had a three-year role, from 1962 until 1965, as half breed blacksmith Quint Asper.

Reynold's portrayal as Quint was understated. He was a soft-spoken loner with a small circle of friends. Quint was stout, a good fighter, and could handle a knife and a gun.

But in spite of his good qualities, producers were not able to decide how best to use Reynolds. He remained mainly in the background, few stories revolved around him, and Quint Asper never developed into a primary character.

Reynolds died in 2018 at age 82.

While Chester Goode and Festus Haggen, and to a lesser degree, Quint Asper, provided Matt with backup, it was the trio of Matt, Miss Kitty, and Doc Adams who were central to the show's success.

Milburn Stone, as Doctor Galen Adams, along with Arness, were the only cast members to stay in Dodge City the entire twenty years. Stone did miss part of the 17th season, however, recovering from heart surgery. Pat Hingle, as Dr. John Chapman, filled in for him.

Doc Adams, as played by Stone, appeared crusty and ill tempered. Underneath, however, he was kind and compassionate. Doc looked after Miss Kitty, and enjoyed an argument with Chester and Festus. Doc Adams was Matt Dillon's best friend. He was a confidant whom Matt looked to for advice. The doctor also dug many a bullet out of the lawman during the show's run.

Stone died in 1980, at the age of 75.

Amanda Blake portrayed Miss Kitty Russell for 19 seasons. In the beginning she was a regular saloon girl. Viewers objected because Kitty had to keep company with any cowhand that came along, so soon she became owner of the Long Branch.

Although she still might pass time with customers, it was apparent that Matt Dillon was the only man in her life.

But to what extent Matt Dillon was in Kitty Russell's life was never fully revealed. There was no doubt the two cared for each other.

After Kitty had been kidnapped, abused, and shot by the Jude Bonner gang in "Hostage," Matt kept a bedside vigil, talking to Kitty, telling her how much he needed her. Then he took off his badge and went after Bonner, intent upon killing him with his bare hands.

After Matt had once again been shot down, in "The Badge," Kitty, thinking she couldn't go through such an ordeal again, left town. She eventually returned.

In the 1987 *Return to Dodge* reunion movie, Kitty again came to Matt's side as he recovered from a knife wound.

Matt Dillon and Kitty Russell kissed only once on screen, a brief peck on Matt's cheek during a Christmas episode. It was left up to the viewers to decide if their relationship went any farther than that.

Amanda Blake passed at age 60, in 1989.

After *Gunsmoke* failed to break the top thirty in ratings for its first season, producer Charles Marquis Warren resigned and Norman Macdonnell was brought in to nurture his creation.

Nurture it he did, as *Gunsmoke* moved to number eight its second season, then began a four-year run as being the number one rated program on television.

A primary factor contributing to *Gunsmoke's* success was the scripts. For most of the first few seasons the television show took stories which had already been used on radio, and adapted them as needed. Many were written by John Meston.

After six seasons as a thirty-minute show, *Gunsmoke* was expanded to one hour in 1961. After a successful initial season of being rated third, the program suffered a gradual loss in viewers.

In 1964, Macdonnell was fired as producer. Phillip Leacock guided the show three seasons, including the 1966 change from black and white to color.

Nothing seemed to help as *Gunsmoke's* ratings continue to decline. The show was cancelled for a two-week period in 1967, before CBS president William S. Paley ordered it renewed. *Gunsmoke* was then moved from Saturday to Monday night, which resulted in a television miracle. *Gunsmoke* again entered the top ten, and stayed there until 1974.

For a time after the move to Monday, *Gunsmoke's* opening was Matt Dillon racing his horse across the prairie. The scene was shot after Arness had learned the show had been cancelled. He spurred the horse, and was clocked doing 30 miles an hour.

CBS replaced Leacock in 1968 with John Mantley. With television violence being toned down because of social issues, rather than fighting CBS censors Mantley changed the program's look.

Gunsmoke began to have more character studies and to incorporate social topics into the scripts. Viewers saw less of Dillon and more of the other stars, and weekly guests. At times Dillon only appeared at the end of an episode, usually to tie up loose ends.

Another supporting character was added, Buck Taylor as Newly O'Brien. Newly, handsome and polite, was a gunsmith and stood ready to ride with Matt and Festus at a moment's notice.

Newly had studied medicine for a time, so he was able to help Doc Adams in a pinch. In the 1987 reunion movie, Newly had gained the title of United States Marshal.

Several secondary characters were introduced and defined over the years, fleshing out Dodge City and becoming a part of the *Gunsmoke* landscape. They included Glenn Strange as Sam the bartender, James Nusser as town drunk Louie Pheeters, and Ted Jordan as freight office manager Nathan Burke.

For two seasons Roger Ewing played Thad Greenwood, a homeless young man befriended by the *Gunsmoke* regulars.

Following the switch to Monday nights for its 13th season, *Gunsmoke* soared from 34th place to 4th. It remained in the top ten until 1974, when it fell to 15th.

After that 19th season Amanda Blake, tired of the commute from her home in Phoenix to Hollywood, quit. She may have returned had the series been renewed for a 21st season.

But she never had the chance. After twenty seasons CBS cancelled *Gunsmoke,* this time for good.

Gunsmoke was still a popular program, finishing in a tie for 26th place. But CBS said it was popular among the wrong type of people. Advertisers wanted shows which were attractive to the young, urban population.

The loyalty of *Gunsmoke,* though, was considered to be primarily rural men over 40 years of age.

Gunsmoke refused to stay dead, and in 1987 the TV movie *Gunsmoke: Return to Dodge* reunited James Arness, Amanda Blake, and Buck Taylor. Rumors of a *Gunsmoke* reunion had abounded for years, and CBS originally projected a 1985 air date. Delays, mostly concerned with obtaining a workable script, pushed the movie back two years.

Other *Gunsmoke* regulars had been unsuccessfully approached about returning. A financial arrangement with Ken Curtis could not be reached. Dennis Weaver was starring in his own series, *Buck James*. Milburn Stone had died.

Burt Reynolds and Roger Ewing, as Quint Asper and Thad Greenwood, were not asked to reprise their roles.

One actor who was asked to revive a *Gunsmoke* character was Steve Forrest, whose return was a key element in the movie's success. Forrest brought back Will Mannon, one of the most memorable villains to appear on the show.

Return to Dodge was well received, and CBS made plans for a second movie.

1990's *The Last Apache* met with more acclaim than the earlier effort. Arness was again back as Dillon. But following Amanda Blake's death in 1989, nothing is said about the other *Gunsmoke* characters and his time in Dodge City is only briefly mentioned.

The Last Apache was built around the 1973 episode, "Matt's Love Story," where Dillon was ambushed, lost his memory, and found himself on the

Yardner Cattle Ranch in Arizona. His memory eventually returned, and he traveled back to Dodge City.

With *The Last Apache* being a success, CBS gave the go ahead for a third movie.

To the Last Man aired in 1992, with Arness the only *Gunsmoke* regular. The setting was again Arizona, far from the dusty streets of Dodge City, Kansas. The movie is based, loosely, on one of the bloodiest feuds in the history of the American West, the Pleasant Valley, Arizona, War of the 1880's. More than 50 settlers were murdered before it ended.

Two more *Gunsmoke* movies followed, 1993's *The Long Ride* and 1994's *One Man's Justice*. As usual, the only tie-in to the series was Arness as the retired marshal, now a rancher in Arizona.

In *The Long Ride*, Dillon has to clear his name of robbery and murder charges before a posse catches him. *One Man's Justice* finds Dillon helping a 15-year-old boy bring his mother's killers to justice.

James Arness, at age 71, still rode tall in the saddle as Matt Dillon in *One Man's Justice*. It had been 39 years since he pinned on the marshal's badge for the first time.

It was something of a miracle Arness had an acting career at all. During World War II, he was walking point on night patrol at Anzio when he was shot in the right leg by a machine gun. He was in a cast eight months, and was hampered in his recovery by osteomyelitis, a bone infection. The limp was never an act.

But Arness was tough. He became a television superstar, and created a character that remains a television legend.

Arness was Matt Dillon. His show ... was *Gunsmoke*.

Made for Television Movies

Return to Dodge, 1987, CBS-TV

The *Gunsmoke* reunion movie – written by Jim Byrnes and directed by Vincent McEveety – stars *Gunsmoke* regulars James Arness, Amanda Blake, and Buck Taylor, with Steve Forrest reprising his Will Mannon character from the "Mannon" episode.

Dillon is retired and living the life of a trapper in the Rocky Mountains. He's waylaid by a gang and stabbed before escaping in a canoe. Dillon awakens in Dodge City with Kitty Russell standing over him.

Meanwhile, Mannon, who managed to survive his earlier shootout with Dillon, is being released from prison and has revenge on his mind.

The resulting story travels hither and yon. Mannon once again takes over Dodge, and again encounters Kitty Russell as he awaits Dillon's arrival. The final climax between Dillon and Mannon is as satisfying as any seen on the series.

Flashbacks from the "Mannon" episode, as well as "The Badge," fleshed out the movie.

The Last Apache, 1990, CBS-TV

James Arness is the only *Gunsmoke* veteran in this entry, which is built around, and has flashbacks from, the 1973 episode, "Matt's Love Story." The story is also based upon the actual decimation of the Apache Nation.

Dillon learns, 21 years after the fact, he is the father of Beth Yardner, whose mother, Mike, he had a brief affair with while recovering from amnesia in Arizona. Before he can get to the Yardner Cattle Ranch and meet his daughter, renegade Apaches kidnap her.

An Army scout, Chalk Brighton, who himself has eyes for Mike, teams up with Dillon to rescue Beth. The trail is winding, and nothing comes easy. Eventually their mission is successful. Dillon makes peace with Wolf, the leader of the renegades who becomes the last free Apache.

This entry – written by Earle Wallace and directed by Charles Correll – is regarded as being the best of the *Gunsmoke* movies.

Michael Learned played Mike Yardner, as she did in the 1973 episode. Richard Kiley is Chalk Brighton, Geoffrey Lewis is Bodine, Joe Lara is Wolf, Joaquin Martinez plays Geronimo, and Beth is played by Amy Stock-Poynton.

To the Last Man, 1992, CBS-TV

Once again using historical fact as a starting point, this movie involves Dillon in one of the bloodiest feuds in the American West, the Pleasant Valley, Arizona, War of the 1880's.

It begins with the burial of Mike Yardner, with Matt and Beth left to carry on. Cattle rustlers soon strike, and the trail leads north, into Pleasant Valley.

James Arness was the only *Gunsmoke* regular. But Morgan Woodward, who guest starred in 18 episodes, was aboard as aged lawman Abel Rose.

Pat Hingle, who filled in as Dodge City's doctor while Milburn Stone recovered from heart surgery, plays Colonel Tucker. Amy Stock-Poynton returns as Beth Yardner. Earle Wallace was again the writer, with the director being Jerry Jameson.

This movie was extremely violent, with Matt Dillon taking it upon himself to regain his stolen cattle and end the war.

With the help of Abel Rose, he succeeds.

The Long Ride, 1993, CBS-TV

The fourth entry in the *Gunsmoke* movie series started with the wedding of Matt Dillon's daughter. But the celebration was interrupted when two bounty hunters show up with a wanted poster for Dillon, dead or alive.

Dillon knew he was being framed and realized his only chance was to find the real criminals, all the while staying one step ahead of a posse.

He's helped, of course, by his daughter and son-in-law, but also by John "the Methodist" Parsley, played by James Brolin, and "Uncle Jane" Merkle, Ali MacGraw.

Amy Stock-Poynton again portrays Beth, and Christopher Bradley is Josh. Bill Stratton was the writer, Jerry Jameson again the director.

As with the movies before it, *The Long Ride* had a high body count. But it's apparent the violence has taken its toll on Dillon, as he wistfully remarks how tired he is of the killing.

In the end, standing over the grave of a friend, the viewer sees the retired marshal reflecting upon his own mortality. Then slowly, even sadly, Matt Dillon mounts his horse, and rides away.

One Man's Justice, 1994, CBS-TV

This fifth installment co-stars Bruce Boxleitner, who starred with Arness in the late 1970's series *How the West Was Won*. Harry and Renee Longstreet were the writers, Jerry Jameson directing for the third time.

Boxleitner plays Davis Haley, a fast-drawing traveling salesman who insists upon helping Dillon track down an outlaw gang who killed a 15-year-old boy's mother. Haley's real motive was eventually revealed.

Kelly Morgan was Lucas Miller, the boy bound for revenge. Amy Stock-Poynton and Christopher Bradley were on board again as Dillon's daughter and son-in-law.

Twenty Episodes to Remember

Season 1 "Matt Gets It" – story by John Meston, Charles Marquis Warren teleplay and director. The first episode, introduced by John Wayne. Dillon challenges fast draw Dan Grat, and is shot down. The marshal, having determined Grat's weakness, recovers and goes after him again.

Season 2 "Bloody Hands" – written by John Meston and directed by Andrew McLaglen. Marshal Dillon, after taking the life of three men in a gunfight, turns in his badge. With an outlaw running amok in Dodge, it's up to Chester to convince Matt to return.

Season 3 "Buffalo Man" – written by John Meston and directed by Les Crutchfield. Buffalo hunters Ben Siple and Earl Ticks are holding Siple's "woman," Abby, against her will. Matt and Chester are themselves captured when they try to rescue her.

Season 4 "The F.U." – written by John Meston and directed by Andrew McLaglen. Clever bank robbers use a decoy to lure Matt and Chester out of Dodge.

Season 5 "The Bobsy Twins" – written by John Meston and directed by Jesse Hibbs. Two crazed, decadent, ignorant hillbilly brothers leave a blood trail of innocent victims as they travel through Kansas intent upon killing Indians. If they can find any.

Season 6 "Unloaded Gun" – written by John Meston and directed by Jesse Hibbs. As a favor to the sick marshal, Chester starts cleaning Dillon's gun. But he's distracted before finishing the job. Dillon is then called upon to face an outlaw while weak, having a fever, and, unknown to him, carrying an empty gun.

Season 7 "The Gallows" – written by John Meston and directed by Andrew McLaglen. One of the series' grimmest episodes. Dillon captures accused murderer Pruit Dover. On the way back to Dodge, Dover saves Matt's life. At the trial, despite there only being circumstantial evidence, and despite Matt's intervention, Dover is sentenced to hang. The marshal then has to escort Dover to Hayes City for his execution.

Season 8 "Anybody Can Kill a Marshal" – written by Kathleen Hite and directed by Harry Harris. Two men decide the easiest way to rob the Dodge City bank is to kill Matt Dillon. After a couple of failures, they wonder if such is possible.

Season 9 "Extradition, Parts 1 & 2" – written by Anthony Ellis and directed by John English. Dillon's first trip into Mexico and the first multi-part episode of the series.

Season 10 "Twenty Miles from Dodge" – written by Clyde Ware and directed by Mark Rydell. Kitty and other passengers on a stagecoach are held for ransom, in the middle of nowhere.

Season 11 "Seven Hours to Dawn," – written by Clyde Ware and directed by Vincent McEveety. An outlaw army takes over Dodge, disarms everyone (including Dillon) and pillages the town.

Season 12 "The Jailer" – written by Hal Sitowitz and directed by Vincent McEveety. Bette Davis shines as vengeful widow Etta Stone, who blames Dillon for her husband's death. Her sons kidnap Kitty, knowing Matt will follow to his hanging.

Season 13 "Baker's Dozen" – written by Charles Stone (brother of Milburn) and directed by Irving Moore. A showcase for Milburn Stone as Doc frantically attempts to find a home for newborn triplets, before they are placed in an orphanage.

Season 14 "Mannon" – written by Ron Bishop and directed by Robert Butler. Will Mannon rides into Dodge and announces to all he's there to kill Matt Dillon. He seems likely to do it, with his draw being the fastest anyone has ever seen. As he awaits Dillon's return, he sets out to conquer the town and everybody in it, including Kitty.

Season 15 "The Badge" – written by Jim Byrnes and directed by Vincent McEveety. After Dillon is shot Doc removes the bullet, telling him it's the eleventh time in fifteen years. Tired of the emotional toll, Kitty puts the Long Branch for sale and leaves.

Season 16 "Chato" – written by Paul Edwards and directed by Vincent McEveety. Filmed on location in New Mexico, Dillon goes after the murderous renegade Chato.

Season 17 "The Bullet, Parts 1, 2, & 3" - written by Jim Byrnes and directed by Bernard McEveety. Doc intends to take Matt by train to Denver where a more qualified surgeon can remove the bullet lodged near Matt's spine. But the train carries a shipment of gold, and has been targeted by outlaws.

Season 18 "Hostage!" – written by Paul Edwards and directed by Gunnar Hellstrom. Hoping to save his brother Virgil from hanging, Jude Bonner and his gang kidnap Kitty. The ploy doesn't work. The gang then abuse Kitty, carry her back to Dodge, and shoot her down. Matt, after a night at Kitty's side, takes off his badge and goes after Bonner.

Season 19 "Matt's Love Story" – written by Ron Bishop and directed by Gunnar Hellstrom. Matt, shot and with amnesia, is taken in by attractive widow Mike Yardner. This episode is the basis for the *Last Apache* movie.

Season 20 "Thirty a Month and Found" – Written by Jim Byrnes and directed by Bernard McEveety. A brilliant lament to the end of a way of life in the Old West, the cattle drive. Tragedy follows tragedy as Dillon and Festus chase three cowboys who fear the coming changes.

Twenty Quotes Worth Repeating

"What doth the Lord require of thee but to do justly, to love mercy, and to walk humble with thy God." (Micah 6:8) – Matt, talking of Ira Shurlock, deceased, who enforced Old Testament teachings through violence in "Kangaroo," written by John Meston.

"You got him, Mister Dillon! I never seen anything so fast in all my life! I thought he never would go down! I about died myself, waiting for him to go down!" – Chester to Matt after he had been forced to kill an old friend: "Hack Prine," written by John Meston.

"He's a killer, Doc. He's got to be eliminated." – Matt to Doc Adams, talking of Crego: "The Killer," story by John Meston, teleplay by John Dunkel.

"Crego, you put that gun on and come out in the street. If you don't, I'm coming back in here. And I'm gonna kill ya!" – Matt, determined to put an end to Crego's legal executions, by any means possible: "The Killer," story by John Meston, teleplay by John Dunkel.

"Want some horehound candy, Mister Dillon?" – Chester to Matt, both horseless in pouring rain watching outlaws escape: "The F.U." written by John Meston.

"You've stumbled into a hornet's nest, marshal." "Looks to me like I hit a gold mine." – The outlaw Hack and Dillon: "The Cabin," written by John Meston.

"I swear I'm no Indian. I'm German!" – Carl the stableman to Merle and Harvey: "The Bobsy Twins," as they tighten the noose around his neck. Written by John Meston.

"I don't know that Dillon was born. He could have just come up full growed one day!" – Cleed telling his thoughts to Lucas: "Anybody Can Kill a Marshal," written by Kathleen Hite.

"I didn't think he had a brain in his head." – Mace Gore, after being outfoxed by Festus: "Seven Hours to Dawn," written by Clyde Ware.

"Kitty, we've never needed explanations, have we?" – Matt to Kitty as she leaves town: "The Badge," written by Jim Byrnes.

"Doc, I just wish there was something I could do to help." "There is." – Festus and Doc as the doctor bows his head over the gravely wounded Kitty Russell: "Hostage," written by Paul Edwards.

"What you aim to do, Dillon? Talk me to death?" "No. I figure on taking you apart with my bare hands!" Jude Bonner and Matt: "Hostage," written by Paul Edwards.

"Most lawmen, they ain't good for nothing but dehorning drunks. But Matt's still an eagle-eyed hell wind." – Luke Brazo: "Lobo," written by Jim Byrnes.

"It's been a lotsa years, Red, and I ain't never lost." "You just did. With me." – Kitty, working on the ego of "Mannon," as he awaits Dillon's return. Written by Ron Bishop.

"How many bullets do you think I've dug out of you over the years, Matt? I'll tell you how many. Eleven. That's how many." – Doc to Matt, after removing a bullet in "The Badge," written by Jim Byrnes.

"You know, I'll bet tomorrow night at this time you're knocking on the pearly gates and hollering up to Saint Peter saying, 'Open up the gates, Saint Peter! I'm the marshal!'" – Lou Stone to an imprisoned Matt: "The Jailer," written by Hal Sitowitz.

"You're nothing, Mannon. All you're good for is beating up on women! Now draw!" – Dillon to Will Mannon: *Return to Dodge*, written by Jim Byrnes.

"If the Lord asked me what kind of daughter I wanted, I sure know what to tell Him." – Matt to his daughter, Beth: *The Last Apache*, written by Earle Wallace.

"Got any preferences, Matt?" "Yeah. Rather you didn't miss." – Abel Rose and Dillon, approaching Colonel Tucker's gang of killers: *To the Last Man*, written by Earle Wallace.

"I guess you can see it clear now, John. You and Jane. Keep that light on for me." – Matt, standing at the graves of his friends, Reverend John Parsley and Jane Merkle: *The Long Ride*, written by Bill Stratton.

Bonanza

1959 – 1973, NBC, 428 episodes all one hour in color.

Cast:

Lorne Greene as Ben Cartwright
Michael Landon as Joseph "Little Joe" Cartwright
Dan Blocker as Eric "Hoss" Cartwright, 1959-1972
Pernell Roberts as Adam Cartwright, 1959-1965
Victor Sen Yung as Hop Sing
David Canary as Candy Cannady, 1967-1970, 1972-1973
Mitch Vogel as Jamie Hunter Cartwright, 1970-1973
Ray Teal as Sheriff Roy Coffee, 1959-1967
Bing Russell as Sheriff Clem Foster, 1967-1973

Ratings:

Season	Rank
1959-60	Not available
1960-61	17th
1961-62	2nd
1962-63	4th
1963-64	2nd
1964-65	1st
1965-66	1st
1966-67	1st
1967-68	4th
1968-69	3rd
1969-70	3rd
1970-71	9th
1971-72	20th
1972-73	48th

This series was created by David Dortort.

The theme songs were composed by David Rose.

Seasons 1 through 11 & 14, "Bonanza;" this driving instrumental reached 19th on the pop charts in 1961. The lyrics – which were not used on the show – were written by Jay Livingston and Ray Evans.

The theme for seasons 12 & 13 was "The Big Bonanza."

Synopsis:

Of the Western series which have appeared on television, *Gunsmoke* is deserving of its position of best ever.

One show is a clear choice for second – *Bonanza,* the saga of the Cartwright family of Virginia City, Nevada.

The story of *Bonanza* is familiar: the tale of Ben Cartwright, three times a widower, carving an empire on the thousand square-mile Ponderosa Ranch in the Sierra Nevada Mountains.

It was the story of his family, his three sons, one born by each wife, each one different – Adam, the intellect; Hoss, the giant, slow to anger with a heart of gold; and Little Joe, feisty, a romantic.

The time period was the years of the Civil War, soon after the discovery of the Comstock Silver Lode in Virginia City. As the series progressed the time frame gradually moved forward, finally settling in the mid 1870's.

The adventures of the Cartwrights, both individually and collectively, their cattle, timber, and mining dealings, and the numerous characters they came into contact with, good and bad, made *Bonanza* a staple of television viewing for more than a decade.

Bonanza was the brainchild of David Dortort. After having produced the TV series *The Restless Gun,* Dortort was hired by NBC to develop and produce an hour-long Western.

Dortort and the network clashed from the beginning. He insisted upon shooting the show in color, making *Bonanza* the first color Western on network television. He wanted nothing to do with dusty cow towns which viewers saw on other Westerns. Rather, Dortort wanted the audience to see the glories of the West, the blue skies, green trees, rolling grasses, clear waters.

His cause may have been aided by the fact that NBC was owned by RCA Television, which was beginning a push towards their color sets.

But the biggest point of contention was that of casting. The network wanted established stars. Dortort said television made its own stars, and cast virtual unknowns in the lead roles.

Dortort also reasoned since men were more likely to watch a Western, the fewer women and children cluttering up the action, the better. Thus, his all-male cast.

Lorne Greene, the radio voice of the Canadian Broadcasting Corporation, became Ben, the father. The sons were Pernell Roberts, a veteran of stage and theater who was not overly familiar on television; Dan Blocker, a New Mexico schoolteacher who had appeared in bit parts on other Westerns; and Michael Landon, the best known of the four.

Landon had recently starred in the movie *I Was a Teenage Werewolf*, and had major roles in the movies *God's Little Acre* and *The Legend of Tom Dooley*.

Dortort's ensemble casting was different than other Westerns of the day, which mainly revolved around one star. By placing the series on a ranch rather than in a town, he avoided the weekly shootout on Main Street.

And, he was able to depict different aspects of Western life, such as ranching and mining, which up until then had largely been ignored on TV Westerns.

The first season, 1959 – 1960, *Bonanza* was shown opposite the popular *Perry Mason* on Saturday nights. It was beaten in the ratings and failed to break the top thirty, but the network didn't want to give up on their investment so soon.

NBC's patience paid off. In year two, *Bonanza* finished right behind *Mason*, in 17th place.

For the 1961 – '62 season *Bonanza* was moved to Sunday night. There it exploded, finishing second in the ratings. *Bonanza* was fourth and second the following two seasons. Then the show began a three-year run as the number one program on television, setting viewing records which stood for more than twenty years.

As *Bonanza* progressed, the tone and style of the show changed. In the early years the Cartwrights considered nearly everyone outside the Ponderosa boundaries as enemies. Eventually they became tolerant of others, becoming involved in the affairs of Virginia City until they were regarded as community leaders. The Ponderosa became willing hosts to wayfaring strangers.

Bonanza was rightfully considered a Western. But it was *Bonanza's* ability to do other types of yarns that set it apart. Love stories, character studies, social issues, and comedy were all done well.

Each of the Cartwrights was featured in numerous individual adventures, and the family history was shown in flashback episodes telling of Ben's three wives.

Ben's first wife, Adam's mother, was Elizabeth Stoddard, played by Geraldine Brooks. Ben and Elizabeth were married in New England, where Adam was born. After she died, Ben and Adam headed West.

Ben met and married Inger Borgstrom in St. Joseph, Missouri. She gave birth to Eric, soon to be known as Hoss, on the Great Plains, where she died. Ben married his third wife, Marie DeMarne, played by Felicia Farr, while on a business trip to New Orleans.

After Little Joe was born, Marie was killed after being thrown from a horse.

It was comedy, however, that *Bonanza* did as well as anything. The comedic talent of Dan Blocker primarily made such episodes possible.

A comedy, in fact, may be *Bonanza's* most popular episode. "Hoss and the Leprechauns," where Hoss tries to convince everyone he really has seen, "little green men," is *Bonanza* at its most humorous.

But no matter what type stories *Bonanza* had, or how well they were written, the show could not have lasted for 14 years and 428 episodes without the four superb actors who portrayed the Cartwrights.

Lorne Greene as Ben was an excellent father figure. He possessed a commanding voice, and played Ben Cartwright as being physically tough, yet compassionate and understanding. Ben had faced tragedy three times in his life, but was strong enough to continue his dream of carving a home on the Ponderosa.

Bonanza was the highlight of Greene's career. Following its cancellation, he starred in three more shows: *Griff, Battlestar Galactica,* and *Code Red.* None approached *Bonanza's* popularity.

In 1987, the 72-year-old Greene had signed to star in the television movie, *Bonanza: the Next Generation.* Before filming started, he underwent surgery for a perforated ulcer. Greene developed pneumonia and died on September 11, before he could once again play Ben Cartwright.

The role of Adam went to Pernell Roberts. The "Cartwright in black" was Ben's right-hand man, steady and serious. He would rather reason with an enemy than fight, but could successfully do both. It was Adam who would have been the controlling force behind the Ponderosa when Ben stepped down.

It wasn't to be, however. Roberts soon tired of the show, and asked to be released from his five-year contract. He complained the hurried shooting schedule required of an hour-long series didn't leave time to properly rehearse, and that three grown sons should be more independent of their father.

Roberts, in turn, was accused of trying to become the show's star, rather than one of four stars. Some thought he was unhappy that his character was proving to be the least popular of the Cartwrights.

Dortort considered having the character marry and start his own family, with Roberts becoming a part-time cast member. In the end, however, neither Dortort nor the network wanted to tinker with their enormous hit.

When his contract expired, Roberts surprised everyone by signing a one-year extension. At the end of that contract he walked away, leaving the number one program on television.

Although *Bonanza* continued to soar in popularity after Roberts left, Dortort left the door open for his return. But gradually the family quit mentioning him, and it finally became as if Adam Cartwright had never existed.

After fourteen years of doing guest appearances, Roberts landed the starring role in *Trapper John, M.D.* The series had a successful six-year run.

Roberts passed in 2010, at the age of 81.

When developing *Bonanza,* David Dortort claims he had Dan Blocker in mind for the middle son. Blocker was a high school teacher in New Mexico, holding a Master's Degree in English. He went to Hollywood, to see if there was any acting work available for a large man who had played Shakespeare on the Texas stage.

Blocker landed some guest spots on several Westerns, and was signed by Dortort. Though inexperienced, Blocker grew into the role. Indeed, it soon became apparent that Dan Blocker's Hoss Cartwright was the heart and soul of *Bonanza*.

Did the script call for straight Western action? Turn Hoss loose. Comedy? Have him come down with spring fever. Can Blocker carry a love story? No problem. Which of the four actors would be best to get a misfit on his feet? Blocker. Hoss fought the bad, sided with the weak, and was a loving son and brother.

In May, 1972, Blocker had gallbladder surgery. During his recovery a blood clot developed in his lung, and Blocker died at the age of 43.

Bonanza lasted only one half of a season following Blocker's death. His loss, combined with the show being moved to Tuesday night from its long-time Sunday time period, was too much for the show to overcome.

Michael Landon, though not a star, had numerous acting credits when he was signed. He relished the part of Little Joe, as the character was able to have more reckless types of adventures than the older, more mature Cartwrights.

Little Joe was quick to fight, quick to fall for a girl, and was always ready to do just about anything. Landon played him to the hilt.

Over the years, viewers saw Landon grow from being a fresh-faced, small-ish twenty-two-year-old to a solid, slightly rugged, graying man of thirty-five. (Landon was grayer during the final years of *Bonanza* than he ever was afterward. He started dyeing his hair soon after the series ended.)

Like Roberts, Landon became restless with the show. But unlike Roberts, who longed for escape, Landon looked for new challenges within *Bonanza* itself.

Under Dortort's guidance, Landon became an accomplished writer and director. More than thirty of *Bonanza's* episodes were written and/or directed by Landon, the majority of them being excellent productions.

Following *Bonanza*, Landon became a television father himself in the highly successful *Little House on the Prairie*. He served as both producer and star of the series, in addition to writing and directing numerous episodes.

In *Highway to Heaven*, Landon scored with his third major hit, an unprecedented achievement. He once again served as producer/director/writer/star, and the series ran five years.

In 1990, Landon and NBC ended a thirty-year relationship when he signed with CBS to develop and star in a series. The show, *Us*, with Landon playing a traveling columnist recently released after 18 years of wrongful imprisonment, had been scheduled for CBS's 1991 fall lineup.

Landon, however, was diagnosed as having inoperable liver and pancreatic cancers in the spring of 1991. On July 1, he died at the age of 54.

When it became apparent Pernell Roberts would be leaving *Bonanza*, producer David Dortort toyed with the idea of replacing him with a similar character. For several episodes in 1965, Guy Williams, formally *Zorro* and soon to be seen as the father in *Lost in Space*, played Will Cartwright, Ben's long-lost nephew.

But Williams didn't mesh as well as Dortort had hoped, and Will Cartwright soon went on his way.

In 1970, Dortort decided the *Bonanza* theme song needed updating. David Rose, who composed the original, wrote a new theme that opened and closed the 12th and 13th seasons.

The show's opening also changed. Instead of the stars riding across a meadow toward the camera, they were shown in brief action and/or comedy sequences.

The original theme returned for the 14th season. The stars were also introduced on horseback again, though in individual clips instead of together.

During the show's fourteen seasons, numerous episodes had the Cartwrights ready to marry only to lose the girl, for whatever reason, in the end. Joe did marry once, in "Forever," but quickly became a widower. Why?

Why wasn't Ben ever allowed to remarry? Or why didn't one, or all three, of the sons marry and have their own family?

Because Dortort wouldn't allow it. Just as he didn't want a Main Street gunfight in every episode, he didn't want *Bonanza* getting bogged down in domestic storylines. Dortort's *Bonanza* was a Western with men running the show, period.

Who did the cooking and cleaning for these men? Hop Sing, of course. Lorne Greene, Michael Landon, and Victor Sen Yung, as Hop Sing, were the three actors who were on *Bonanza* from the first day to the last. Hop Sing was devoted to his "Cart-lights," and their interaction helped give the program its family warmth.

Several other actors had recurring roles. David Canary was ranch foreman Candy Cannady for four seasons. He had been a wanderer with a quick temper, and got away with rough housing tactics which the Cartwrights might get criticized for.

Ray Teal played Sheriff Roy Coffee for eight years, until Bing Russell took over as Sheriff Clem Foster. Lou Frizzell was Ben's friend Dusty Rhoades for two seasons, and Tim Matheson was convict-turned-ranch hand Griff King during the last season.

A trivia question: who was Ben's youngest son? The answer: Jamie Hunter Cartwright.

In 1970, the 12th season, Dortort decided the show needed an injection of youth to attract younger viewers. With Hoss and Joe grown men, Ben needed someone for whom to be a guiding father figure. So, Dortort brought in Mitch Vogel to play Jamie Hunter, the teen-aged orphaned son of a rainmaker, and landed him at the Cartwright's doorstep.

They took him in, and in "A Home for Jamie," Ben adopted him. Vogel's addition made new types of storylines possible, and Jamie soon became an established character.

After its three seasons at number one, *Bonanza* slipped to 6th in the 1968 ratings. It improved to third in both 1969 and 1970, but fell to ninth in 1971. In its 13th season, *Bonanza* dropped to 20th.

NBC, hoping that a different night and an earlier time slot would attract new viewers (like *Gunsmoke* in 1967), moved the show from its traditional 9 p.m. Sundays to 8 p.m. Tuesdays. The main competition would come from CBS, where *Maude*, a new comedy spun off from the top rated *All in the Family*, would lead in to the popular *Hawaii Five-O*.

In the summer of 1972, *Bonanza* went into syndication under the title *Ponderosa*. Stations jumped at the opportunity to add such a long-standing hit to their programming schedule, resulting in the Cartwrights being on the air every day of the week.

Such saturation couldn't help *Bonanza's* chances entering its 14th season. And when Dan Blocker unexpectedly died, its future was all but certain.

A large audience tuned in for "Forever," the two-hour special which opened *Bonanza's* 14th season. The episode, written and directed by Landon, mentioned the death of Hoss. But Little Joe was finally going to marry, the promotions promised. Maybe everything would be all right.

It was, for a while. Joe married Alice Harper, played by Bonnie Bedelia. She became pregnant. Then she was murdered.

Having to deal with both the passing of Hoss, along with Joe's tragedy, was too much. The audience left in droves. *Maude* caught fire. *Hawaii Five-O* was as strong as ever. And in November, 1972, NBC announced the cancellation of *Bonanza*. The last episode, "The Hunter," aired January 23, 1973.

Bonanza, with its 14 seasons, is the second-longest running network Western behind *Gunsmoke's* 20. And among network shows, its 428 episodes are second to *Gunsmoke's* 635.

The family atmosphere, the scenery, the wide variety of stories possible within the show's framework, and the actors themselves, made *Bonanza* one of the most popular television series ever.

In the mid 1980's, Dortort decided to return to the Ponderosa with the syndicated movie, *Bonanza: the Next Generation*.

The project was not a success. Lorne Greene was the only series star set to return, but he died before filming began.

The only actor remotely connected with the original was Michael Landon, Jr., who played Little Joe's son.

Not to be deterred, Dortort began making plans for a weekly one-hour syndicated series, *Bonanza: Legends of the Ponderosa*. The show didn't develop. But NBC, liking the concept, gave the go-ahead for a two-hour movie using the same cast.

Bonanza: The Return featured the children of Adam, Hoss, and Little Joe. After several years of being separated, they reunited at the Ponderosa during a crisis.

Alistair MacDougall played Adam Jr., Brian Leckner was Hoss's unknown son, Josh, and Little Joe's children were Benji, portrayed by Michael Landon Jr., and Emily Warfield as Sara.

Ben Johnson played Bronc Evans, the man a dying Ben Cartwright appointed to oversee the Ponderosa. Richard Roundtree was foreman Jacob Briscoe, and Dan Blocker's son, Dirk, had a small role as a reporter. Flashbacks helped to establish a continuity with the original series.

Bonanza: The Return was well received. It aired November 28, 1993, and was preceded by a series retrospective, *Back to Bonanza*, hosted by Michael Landon Jr. and Dirk Blocker.

On January 22, 1995, NBC returned to the Ponderosa with *Bonanza II: Under Attack*. This movie, featuring Leonard Nimoy as Frank James, was excellent. Jeff Phillips took the role of Adam Jr., while other "regulars" from *Return* reprised their roles.

Earlier, on September 17, 1991, scenes from *Bonanza* were used when NBC presented *Memories with Love and Laughter, a Tribute to Michael Landon*. The special, hosted by Michael Landon, Jr., featured clips from Landon's movies and television series, along with comments by actors who had guest starred on his shows.

Bonanza, with its reruns, specials, and movies, remained popular years after the show ended in 1973. It was the story of a family with a clear sense of right and wrong, told against the setting of the American West in all its color, with humor and romance added for flavor.

It was the story of the Cartwrights of Nevada. And it was, a *Bonanza*.

Episodes Which Became Movies

Ride the Wind

This two-part story from 1966, in which the Cartwrights become involved in the Pony Express, was released overseas as a movie.

Bonanza – the Movie

Producers took two episodes revolving around persecuted female psychics, 1966's "The Strange One" and 1971's "Second Sight," tied the stories together with a narrator, and released it as a cable movie.

Bonanza Forever

This is the two-hour "Forever" episode which opened the show's final season. Written and directed by Michael Landon, the original script had Hoss marrying Alice Harper. Later in the season, in keeping with tradition, she was to die.

With Blocker's death the story was changed to have Joe marry, with his expectant wife dying during the expanded second hour. Hoss's death was mentioned.

Landon is superb carrying the full load, and the show itself is a top flight tear-jerker.

Made for Television Movies

Bonanza: The Next Generation, 1988, Syndicated

Story by David Dortort, script by Paul Savage, directed by William F. Claxton.

Dortort's attempted reunion movie had numerous obstacles to overcome. Lorne Greene was the only regular set to return. Michael Landon, involved in *Highway to Heaven,* was unavailable. David Canary was busy playing twins in the daytime soap opera, *All My Children.* Pernell Roberts and Mitch Vogel were not asked.

Faced with such a shortage, Dortort brought the Cartwright's "next generation" into play. Michael Landon Jr. would play Joe's son, Benj. Brian A. Smith would play the son no one knew Hoss had fathered, Josh. Joe's absence was explained by having him missing in the Spanish/American War. Barbara Anderson was Joe's wife, Annabelle.

Robert Fuller was ranch foreman Charlie Polk. John Amos was handyman Mister Mack. For a conflict, a mining company was using illegal methods to unearth Ponderosa silver. Filming was to begin at Lake Tahoe in October, 1987.

When Greene passed, the only direct tie-in with the series was severed. Hoping to establish some continuity, Dortort created Ben's brother, Aaron. Played by veteran Western actor John Ireland, Aaron became the movie's father figure and the Ponderosa's guiding hand.

The movie's restraints, including being aired at odd times on various cable channels, proved too much to overcome.

Bonanza: The Return, 1993, NBC-TV

Story by Michael McGreevey, Tom Brinson, and Michael Landon Jr., script by McGreevey, directed by Jerry Jameson.

Taking the best ideas from the *Next Generation* movie, adding concepts from the planned *Legends of the Ponderosa* series which never aired, and with the backing of NBC, this is a game attempt to return viewers to the Ponderosa.

Viewers are expected to forget *The Next Generation,* whose setting was 1907. *The Return* is set in 1905.

Ben and Hoss Cartwright are dead and buried on the Ponderosa. Joe died a war hero in the Spanish/American War, and is buried in the Arlington National Cemetery. Adam is settled in Australia. An old friend of Ben's, Bronc Evans, runs the Ponderosa, assisted by foreman Jacob Briscoe.

Long-time cowboy actor Ben Johnson plays Bronc. Helping his cause is a scene from the series featuring Johnson and Lorne Greene. Richard Roundtree is Jacob. Veteran Western actor Jack Elam is Buckshot, the cook.

Returning from *The Next Generation* is Michael Landon Jr. as Joe's son, Benj. The character of Josh is also reprised, with Brian Leckner taking over as the son of Hoss. New offspring are Adam Jr., the black-haired Alistair MacDougall, and Joe's daughter Sara, played by Emily Warfield.

Dirk Blocker is included as a reporter, Linda Gray is a saloon girl/informer, and Dean Stockwell is the vengeful Augustus Brandenburg, who was shot and crippled by Ben years ago.

Ben's grandchildren are scattered. But when they learn Brandenburg plans to take over the Ponderosa, they come running. The offer to sell is tempting – five million dollars. But inspired by flashbacks from the original series, the grandchildren combine to thwart the takeover attempt.

Bonanza II: Under Attack, 1995, NBC-TV

Written by Denne Bart Petitclerc, directed by Mark Tinker.

With the success of *The Return*, NBC gave the go-ahead for the superior *Under Attack*.

Ben Johnson, Richard Roundtree, Michael Landon Jr., Emily Warfield, Brian Leckner, and Jack Elam returned from the first offering, with Jeff Phillips taking the role of Adam Jr.

Leonard Nimoy, as reformed outlaw Frank James, contributed greatly to the movie's success. James seeks help from a renegade Pinkerton by looking up his Civil War buddy, Ben Johnson's Bronc.

Gunfights, a strong sense of family, bits of humor, love interests for Bronc and Adam Jr., location filming, and a literate script by Denne Bart Petitclerc, make *Under Attack* an enjoyable outing.

The *Ponderosa* Series

At the age of 84, David Dortort returned to his beloved Cartwrights with *Ponderosa*. This prequel to *Bonanza* aired during the 2001-2002 season on PAX-TV.

Set in 1849, the series centered around the beginning of Ben's ranch. He was played by Daniel Hugh Kelly. Teen-agers Adam and Hoss were portrayed by Matt Carmody and Drew Powell. Jared Daperis was young Little Joe. Filmed in Australia, the show aired twenty episodes.

Novels of Note

Numerous fictional books based upon Western television series have been written. Most were published when the shows originally aired, and were targeted for both children, and general audiences. *Gunsmoke* and *Bonanza* also offered paperbacks, more than thirty years later.

Of all these books, two were superior. Based upon *Bonanza*, they were published in 1966 and 1967 by NBC and Media Books, and placed the Cartwrights in the true historical setting of early Virginia City, Nevada.

The first, *Bonanza: One Man with Courage*, was written by Thomas Thompson, a two-time winner of the Silver Spur Award. He wrote several *Bonanza* episodes, and at times served as both story editor and executive producer.

The second book, *Bonanza: Black Silver*, was by William R. Cox. He scripted several episodes, and was a versatile, prolific writer.

The Singing Cartwrights

In addition to their thespian abilities the four *Bonanza* leads were singers. Greene and Roberts, in particular, were gifted.

The foursome performed on the LPs *Bonanza: Ponderosa Party Time*, and *Bonanza: Christmas on the Ponderosa*. Highlights included Greene's "Ponderosa," "My Sons, My Son," and "The Place Where I Worship;" Roberts's "Early One Morning," and "In the Pines;" Blocker's "The Hanging Blues" and "Sky Ball Paint;" and Landon's "Shenandoah" and "Santa Got Lost in Texas."

Greene recorded six individual albums. Songs of note included: "The Man," "Ringo," "An' Ol' Tin Cup," and "Tumbling Tumbleweeds."

Roberts's album of folk music, *Come All Ye Fair and Tender Ladies*, was considered a standard, led by the title track, "Alberta" and "They Call the Wind Maria."

Blocker teamed with John Mitchum for *Our Land, Our Heritage*, which included "Battle Hymn of the Republic" and "Paiute Sunrise Chant." Landon had the singles "Gimme a Little Kiss"/"Be Patient with Me," and "Linda is Lonesome"/"Without You."

Fourteen *Bonanza* Episodes Worth Remembering

Season 1 "A Rose for Lotta" – Written by David Dortort, directed by Edward Ludwig. The first episode. Greedy Virginia City miners, lusting after

Ponderosa timber, hire beautiful Lotta Crabtree to lure Little Joe into town to kidnap so they can strike a deal with Ben.

Season 2 "The Gift" – Written by Thomas Thompson and Demme Bart Petitclerk, directed by William Witney. The half-brothers decide upon a white stallion for their father's birthday. Little Joe, bringing the animal home, runs into a gang of Comancheros.

Season 3 "The Crucible" – Written by John Dugan and directed by Paul Nickell. Pernell Roberts shines as Adam, made to be a human pack animal for a crazed miner (played by Lee Marvin) in a harsh wasteland. One of *Bonanza's* highest rated episodes.

Season 4 "My Brother's Keeper" – Written by Seeleg Lester, directed by Murray Golden. Little Joe's life is in danger after being accidentally shot by Adam.

Season 5 "The Legacy" – Written by Anthony Wilson and directed by Bernard McEveety. After Ben is missing and presumed dead, Adam, Hoss, and Joe split to search for the three men they believe responsible.

Season 6 "To Own the World" – Written by Edward Adamson, directed by Virgil Vogel. One of the world's richest men sets his sights on the Ponderosa.

Season 7 "Ride the Wind" parts 1 & 2 – Written by Paul Schneider and directed by William Witney. The show's first two-part episode features the Pony Express.

Season 8 "Joe Cartwright, Detective" – Story by Oliver Crawford, script by Michael Landon, directed by William F. Claxton. Hilarious episode with Joe, mesmerized by a dime novel, enlisting Hoss to head off a bank robbery.

Season 9 "To Die in Darkness" – Written and directed by Michael Landon (his directorial debut). Ben and Candy, trapped in a large, man-made hole in an abandoned mine, are given up for dead by Hoss and Joe.

Season 10 "A Ride in the Sun" – Written by Peter Germano and directed by Leon Benson. Joe takes off after three men who rob the bank and shoot Ben in the back.

Season 11 "Matter of Circumstance" – Written by B.W. Sandefur and directed by William F. Claxton. Joe, stomped by a horse, attempts to amputate his own arm.

Season 12 "Kingdom of Fear" – Written by Michael Landon and directed by Joseph Pevney. Ben, Hoss, Joe, and Candy are taken captive in a remote forced labor camp. This episode was filmed four years earlier. David Canary's Candy, long gone, simply appears.

Season 13 "Shanklin" – Written by William Kelley and directed by Leo Penn. The Ponderosa is taken over by a gang of former Confederate soldiers. The leader, who is a doctor, shoots Hoss then operates to save his life.

Season 14 "Forever" – Written and directed by Michael Landon. The two-hour opening of the final season. Joe and Alice Harper marry. But her brother's wasteful life comes back to haunt Alice, and she's murdered.

Fourteen *Bonanza* Quotes Worth Repeating

"Look at it, Adam! Feast thine eyes on a sight that approaches Heaven itself!" – Ben to Adam, the first words ever spoken on the series, as they look down on Lake Tahoe: "A Rose for Lotta," written by Dortort.

"You're hurting my arm!" "I'll break it! Where's the kid?" – Lotta Crabtree and Adam Cartwright who is trying to find Little Joe: "A Rose for Lotta," written by Dortort.

"You sold my Pa? How much did you get for him?" – Hoss to Quick Buck Katie: "San Francisco," written by Thomas Thompson.

"Some folks have a natural mean streak animals don't know nothing about." – Hoss: "The Newcomers," written by Thomas Thompson.

"Don't you see, Pa? This house isn't big enough for Joe and me anymore. And he needs you more than I do!" – Adam to his father as he's leaving: "A House Divided," written by Al Ward.

"You heard Pa! We have to look for little green men riding on hound dogs!" – Adam to Little Joe: "Hoss And the Leprechauns," written by Robert Barron.

"Adam's been dragging a dead man, Pa." – Hoss, looking at what his brother had been hauling: "The Crucible," written by John Dugan.

"Dadburn your ornery hide, Little Joe. I'll never listen to you again!" – Hoss to Joe, how many times?

"I'll break it!" "Hoss, don't break it!" "Huh? Oh, hi, Pa!" – Hoss and Joe, as Hoss sits on Ben, holding Ben's leg in a twist: "Joe Cartwright, Detective," story by Oliver Crawford, script by Michael Landon.

"Bread and water for Mister Hoss, Little Joe, bread and water for Mister Cart-light!" – Hop Sing serving Ben his supper as Ben lets his sons spend the night in jail: "Joe Cartwright, Detective," story by Oliver Crawford, script by Michael Landon.

"You sic them dogs on me, mister, I'll kill them." – Hoss to the leader of the "Kingdom of Fear," written by Michael Landon.

"I keep expecting that front door to open and he'll be standing there, like nothing ever happened." – Hoss to Joe, after their father has been missing for a month: "To Die in Darkness," written by Michael Landon.

"I didn't pick my sons; they were born to me. But I did pick you. I didn't have to, but I did." – Ben to Jamie: "The Gold-Plated Rifle," written by Preston Wood.

"You really loved him, didn't you?" "Everybody did. He was that kind of a guy." – Alice Harper and Joe, talking about Hoss: "Forever," written by Michael Landon.

Sixteen Shows Which Lasted Five Years or More

Cheyenne

1955 – 1963, ABC, 107 episodes all one-hour black & white.

Cast:

Clint Walker as Cheyenne Bodie L.Q. Jones as Smitty (1955-1956). Best Ratings: 12th in 1958, 17th in 1960, 18th in 1959.

This program was developed by William Orr and Roy Huggins. The theme song was composed by William Lava. The lyrics by Stan Jones were introduced in season two, with the performer uncredited.

Synopsis:

Clint Walker became a star in this show, set in the vastness of the entire Old West.

Walker – a large, powerful man – played Cheyenne Bodie, a former scout who roamed the West after the Civil War. Bodie had a partner the first season, L. Q. Jones as Smitty, but after that was a loner.

Cheyenne had solid, action-packed stories, but only turned out 107 episodes during 8 seasons. *Wagon Train*, in contrast, had 253 episodes during the same number of years.

The reason for the relative low number of episodes was the off-screen struggles between Walker and Warner Brothers Studio, which owned the show. Walker became unhappy with his contract and felt he was becoming typecast.

The result was that *Cheyenne* was rarely seen on a weekly basis. It first was one of three rotating shows on *Warner Brothers Presents*. Later it alternated, at different times, with *Conflict, Sugarfoot, Bronco,* and *Shirley Temple's Storybook. Cheyenne* was finally weekly during its last season, when many episodes were reruns.

In 1991 Walker reprised the character of Cheyenne Bodie in the Kenny Rogers mini-series, *The Gambler Returns: The Luck of the Draw*.

Rogers, playing Brady Hawks in his fourth *Gambler* production, met several Western TV characters as he traveled to San Francisco for a poker game.

Walked died in 2018, at the age of 90.

Death Valley Days

1952 – 1972, Syndicated, 532 episodes all thirty minutes black & white.

This show was based upon a radio program of the same name, created by Ruth Woodman. The theme song was composed by Herbert Taylor.

Narrators: Stanley Andrews (The "Old Ranger"), Ronald Reagan, Robert Taylor, and Dale Robertson.

Synopsis:

Death Valley Days told stories of the Old West. The episodes were self-contained, never had the same characters twice, were often set in the harsh Death Valley desert region of Southern California, were often filmed on location, and were, for the most part, solid tales of Western characters and adventures.

With its twenty seasons on the air, *Death Valley Days* tied *Gunsmoke* as the longest running Western series.

But where *Gunsmoke* ran all twenty years on CBS and had continuing characters, *Death Valley Days* was a syndicated anthology show.

The traditional opening for *Death Valley Days* was a twenty-mule team hauling borax from the desert. Borax was mined from Death Valley, and the show's long-time sponsor was Twenty Mule Team Borax.

Dick Powell's Zane Grey Theater

1956 – 1962, CBS, 145 episodes all thirty minutes black & white.

Hosted by Dick Powell.

Best Ratings: 13th in 1959, 21st in 1958 and 1960.

This program was created by Luke Short and Charles Wallace. The theme song was composed by Joseph Mullendore.

Synopsis:

Dick Powell's Zane Grey Theater served up six years of black and white, self-contained episodes of Western adventure. Powell, the host, starred in several episodes.

For the first few years the shows were adaptations of the short stories and novels of famed Western author Zane Grey.

When that material began to run out, stories from other authors were included.

The Western television series *Black Saddle, The Rifleman, Johnny Ringo, The Westerner,* and *Trackdown* had their pilot episodes on *Dick Powell's Zane Grey Theater.*

Have Gun Will Travel

1957 – 1963 CBS, 225 episodes all thirty minutes black & white.

Cast:

Richard Boone as Paladin
Kam Tong as Heyboy (1957-1960, 1961-1963)
Lisa Lu as Heygirl (1960-1961)

Best Ratings: 3rd in 1959, 1960, and 1961; 4th in 1958. *Have Gun Will Travel* is the only Western to be rated in the top thirty every season it was on the air.

This series was created by Sam Rolfe and Herb Meadow. (*Have Gun Will Travel* is one of the few television shows which spun off a radio program, which lasted 1958 – '60.) The theme song was composed by Bernard Herrmann. The lyrics were by Johnny Western, Richard Boone, and Sam Rolfe, and performed by Western. The song was a hit single in the early 1960s.

Synopsis:

The premise of *Have Gun Will Travel* was simple. A man who called himself Paladin had a gun for hire. Pay his price, and the gun would do your bidding.

Actor Richard Boone developed Paladin into an interesting, complex character, with the program one of the best Westerns to appear on television.

Paladin was the most literate character in Western television. He was college educated, having attended West Point. After the Civil War he went West to hire out his fast gun. Paladin lived the high life in San Francisco's Hotel Carlton in between jobs.

Unlike anyone else of the genre, Paladin had a business card. It bore the figure of a white chess knight, the paladin. The inscription read, "Have Gun, Will Travel. Wire Paladin, San Francisco."

The word paladin means "heroic champion." That, more than anything, describes the character of Paladin. Dressed completely in black, Paladin approached his assignments with caution and cynicism.

If his employer had been wronged, if the cause was just, Paladin did what he was hired to do. But if Paladin's client was a crook himself, Paladin did not hesitate to serve the just dessert.

Boone also directed 27 episodes, and had a large amount of control over writing and production.

He died in 1981, at the age of 63.

Maverick

1957 – 1962 ABC, 124 episodes all one-hour black & white.

Cast:

James Garner as Bret Maverick (1957-1960)
Jack Kelly as Bart Maverick
Roger Moore as Beauregard Maverick (1960-1961)

Best Ratings: 6th in 1959, 19th in 1960.

This series was created by Roy Huggins. The theme song was composed by Paul Buttolph. The lyrics were added late in season two by Paul Frances Webster and performed by an uncredited male chorus.

Synopsis:

Maverick was intended to be a traditional Western show centered around James Garner as professional gambler Bret Maverick. But humor soon found its way into scenes with Garner, and creator Roy Huggins realized the gem he had.

Maverick was somewhat of a maverick in early adult Westerns – a series with laughs, twisting stories, immensely likeable characters, and a gunfight once in a while.

Garner played Bret Maverick as a crafty, card playing ladies' man. When the show became unable to turn out an episode each week, Jack Kelly was added as brother Bart, who was slightly straighter than Bret.

The two sometimes appeared together, but most often alternated leads. Their adventures took them to such towns as Oblivion, Apocalypse, and

Hound Dog. They never strayed far from their "Old Pappy's" advice and preferred to talk their way out of trouble, or even run from it, than meet it head on.

The best remembered *Maverick* episodes might be takeoffs on other popular Westerns. "Three Queens Full" took place on the Subrosa Ranch where Joe Wheelwright was trying to marry off his three sons, Henry, Moose, and Small Paul. And "Hadley's Hunters" had guest appearances by other Warner Brothers stars: Clint *Cheyenne* Walker, John Russell and Peter Brown of *Lawman*, Will *Sugarfoot* Hutchins, Ty *Bronco* Hardin, and even Edd "Kookie" Byrnes from *77 Sunset Strip*.

Garner played Bret Maverick three years before quitting in a contract dispute. In 1981 in reprised the character in the brief NBC series *Bret Maverick* and in 1994 he played "Pappy" in Mel Gibson's big screen *Maverick*.

Garner was replaced on the series by cousin Beauregard Maverick, played by future 007 Roger Moore. On hand for one season were Diane Brewster as con lady Samantha Crawford, and Robert Colbert as cousin Brent.

Jack Kelly stayed for the entire run, and returned as Bart in *The Gambler Returns: The Luck of the Draw*, the 1991 mini-series starring Kenny Rogers. Kelly died a year later at age 65.

Garner passed in 2014 at the age of 86, Moore died at age 89, in 2017.

Rawhide

1959 – 1966 CBS, 144 episodes all one-hour black & white.

Cast:

Clint Eastwood as Rowdy Yates
Eric Fleming as Gil Favor (1959-1965)
Paul Brinegar as Wishbone
Sheb Wooley as Pete Nolan (1959-1965)
James Murdock as Mushy (1959-1965)

Best Ratings: 6th in 1961, 13th in 1962, 18th in 1960.

Rawhide was based upon the 1958 movie, *Cattle Empire*, and the Borden Chase novel, *Chisholm Trail*. The theme was composed by Dimitri Tiomkin with lyrics by Ned Washington and performed by Frankie Laine.

Synopsis:

Rawhide told the story of a cattle drive from Texas to Kansas, and everything that happened along the way.

The program is one of the all-time great Westerns, featuring strong acting, generally excellent stories with a realistic Western feel, and had *the* Western theme song, performed by Frankie Laine.

Charles Marquis Warren, who guided *Gunsmoke* through its first season on television, served as producer for the show.

Rawhide was similar to another classic Western, *Wagon Train,* in that the premise of both was based on actual Western events – in this case a cattle drive.

Guest stars played characters the drovers encountered along the route. And like *Wagon Train, Rawhide* had a couple of outstanding lead actors to build the show around.

Eric Fleming played trail boss Gil Favor. Stout, tight lipped, stubborn, he had the loyalty and respect of his crew, with the men calling him "Boss," or "Mr. Favor."

Favor's right-hand man, his "ramrod," was Rowdy Yates, played by future movie superstar Clint Eastwood. Eastwood's performance was low key, and his character at times appeared somewhat vulnerable.

Paul Brinegar as trail cook, Wishbone, was outstanding in a secondary role. In 1991 Brinegar appeared in Kenny Rogers's *The Gambler Returns: The Luck of the Draw.* He performed twice during 1994, in the big screen *Maverick* and in Hugh O'Brian's television movie, *Wyatt Earp: Return to Tombstone.*

After six seasons, with Eastwood becoming a movie star with his *Man with No Name* motion pictures, Fleming left the show. He signed to make a movie in South America, and drowned during its filming at age 41.

With Gil Favor gone, Rowdy Yates got his own herd together and started North. They never arrived, as *Rawhide* was cancelled January, 1966.

Brinegar died in 1995 at age 77; Wooley in 2003 at age 82, Murdock in 1981 at age 50.

Tales of Wells Fargo

1957 – 1962, NBC, 200 episodes (165 thirty minutes black & white, 35 sixty minutes color).

Cast:

Dale Robertson as Jim Hardie

Best Ratings: 3rd in 1958, 7th in 1959.

This series was created by James Brooks, Frank Gruber, and Gene Reynolds. The theme song was composed by Stanley Wilson.

Synopsis:

Tales of Wells Fargo followed the adventures of Wells Fargo troubleshooter Jim Hardie as he traveled the West, solving problems for the Wells Fargo Transport Company. The problems, of course, mostly involved outlaws and crooked company men.

Hardie could outwit the company men, and outfight or outshoot the others. Quick with his gun, Hardie could stake a claim as being one of the fastest left-handers in the television West.

Dale Robertson, as Hardie, brought body mannerisms and a drawling style of speech to make his character a notch above many others of his day. An excellent horseman, Hardie rode his own "Jubilee" in the show.

During the first four seasons, Hardie was a loner. In the final season, in an effort to revive fallen ratings, the show was expanded to one hour in color, and Hardie purchased a ranch near San Francisco.

Beau McCloud, played by Jack Ging, was his assistant, and William Demarest was ranch foreman Jeb Gaine. Virginia Christine was next door widow rancher Ovie, and her daughters were Mary Jane Saunders as Mary Gee and Lorie Patrick as Tina.

Robertson died in 2013, at the age of 89.

The Adventures of Rin Tin Tin

1954 – 1959, ABC, 164 episodes all thirty minutes black & white.

Cast:

Lee Aaker as Cpl. Rusty
James Brown as Lt. Ripley Masters

Best Rating: 23rd in 1954.

This program was derived from radio programs featuring a German Shepherd dog named Rin Tin Tin which were broadcast from 1930 until 1955. These programs had been inspired by 27 motion pictures in which the animal appeared, from 1922 until 1931. The theme song was taken from the radio programs.

Synopsis:

Rin Tin Tin and his master, Rusty, were the only survivors of an Indian raid. They were taken in by Lt. Ripley Masters of the 101st Cavalry, stationed at Fort Apache, Arizona.

Rusty was soon made honorary corporal, and each week Rusty, "Rinty," and the 101st teamed up to stop trouble.

With its five-year run, *The Adventures of Rin Tin Tin* was quite successful.

Following his career as a child actor, Lee Aaker did not perform again. James Brown died in 1992, at age 72.

The Cisco Kid

1950 – 1956, Syndicated, 156 episodes all thirty minutes color.

Cast:

Duncan Renaldo as Cisco
Leo Carrillo as Pancho

The Cisco Kid had its origin in a short story by O. Henry. It then became a comic strip, a radio series, silent and talking movies, and finally a television show.

Synopsis:

The Cisco Kid, with its 156 episodes, is second only to *The Lone Ranger* as a successful "pre-adult" western.

Cisco and his side-kick, Pancho, rode the America-Mexico border of the late 1800's. They fought for justice in spite of usually being greeted with doubt. The program was entertaining, with Pancho adding humor.

During the fourth season, Renaldo suffered a severe neck injury during filming. Production continued during his hospital stay by filming his double in long shots and from behind, with Renaldo reading his lines from the hospital bed, which were then looped in. Footage from previous episodes was also used.

The Cisco Kid was filmed in color, even though there were virtually no color television sets to receive it.

The producers were looking to the time when color sets would be plentiful. Stations looking for programming would then be more likely to buy *The Cisco Kid*, in color, than another black and white show which looked outdated.

Renaldo died in 1980 at age 76.

Carrillo, who was age 69 when the series began, died in 1961 at age 80.

The Gene Autry Show

1950 – 1956, CBS, 86 episodes (71 black & white, 15 color) all thirty minutes.

Cast:

Gene Autry and Pat Buttram

The theme song, "Back in the Saddle Again," was written by Autry and Ray Whitley, and performed by Autry.

Synopsis:

Singing cowboy Gene Autry, star of Western movies in the 1930's and '40's, came to television in 1950 for a successful six-year run. He was the first Western movie star to appear in a regular television series.

Autry, his horse Champion, and his sidekick, Pat, wandered the Old West fighting injustice. They played different characters each week, in different locales. Autry made sure to sing often, and the show's theme, "Back in the Saddle Again," is a classic.

In making the transition from motion pictures to television, Autry and his production crew devised different angles of filming so as to better depict the action on a television set, rather than what had been used on the big screen.

Autry died at age 91, in 1998. Buttram, who later became Mister Haney on *Green Acres*, died in 1994 at age 78.

The Life and Legend of Wyatt Earp

1955 – 1961, ABC, 226 episodes all thirty minutes black & white.

Cast:

Hugh O'Brian as Wyatt Earp
Lloyd Corrigan as Ned Buntline
Paul Brinegar as Jim "Dog" Kelly (1956-1958)
Douglas Fowley as Doc Holliday (1957-1961)
Dirk London as Morgan Earp (1959-1961)

John Anderson as Virgil Earp (1959-1961)
Trevor Bardette as Ike Clanton (1959-1961)
Morgan Woodward as Deputy "Shotgun" Gibbs (1958-1961)

Best Ratings: 6th in 1958, 10th in 1959, 18th in 1957, 20th in 1960.

The theme song for this program was composed by Harry Warren, with lyrics by Harold Adamson. The song was performed by the Ken Darby Singers.

Synopsis:

This successful series was based upon the life and legend of famed Old West lawman Wyatt Earp, who survived the OK Corral to die in 1929 of old age in Los Angeles.

Standing six feet tall and weighing 175 pounds, star Hugh O'Brian was Earp's physical equal.

This show was unique in that it followed a specific time frame in Earp's life, from his becoming a marshal in the premier episode to the climatic shootout at the OK Corral six years later.

Earp was marshal in Ellsworth, Kansas for the first season, when Ned Buntline presented him with a Buntline Special pistol, which had a twelve-inch barrel. Earp was the marshal in Dodge City for the next three years.

During the final two seasons he was in Tombstone, Arizona, for a long struggle with the Ike Clanton gang.

The Life and Legend of Wyatt Earp ran on ABC from 1955 until 1961, always airing at 8:30 on Tuesday nights. Its 226 episodes are fifth-highest among all the television Westerns.

O'Brian reprised the character in the 1994 television movie, *Wyatt Earp: Return to Tombstone*, which made liberal use of colorized flashbacks.

O'Brian also appeared as Earp in two episodes of the CBS Series, *Paradise*, and in the previously mentioned *The Gambler Returns: The Luck of the Draw*, featuring Kenny Rogers.

He died at age 91, in 2016.

The Lone Ranger

1949 – 1957, ABC, all thirty-minute episodes: 182 black & white, 39 color. Seasons three, five, and seven were entirely reruns. Reruns were also broadcast from 1957 until 1961.

Cast:

Clayton Moore as the Lone Ranger in seasons one, two, three, six, seven, and eight.

John Hart as the Lone Ranger in seasons four and five.

Jay Silverheels as Tonto

Best Ratings: 7th in 1951, 18th in 1952.

The Lone Ranger was based upon the radio program of the same name which lasted 16 years and was created by George Trendle and Fran Strikers. The theme song is one of the most recognizable instrumentals in television history – the dynamic "William Tell Overture." It is the overture (introduction) to the opera, *William Tell*, composed by Gioachino Rossini in 1829.

Synopsis:

Before the wave of "Adult Westerns" hit television, Western television consisted of shows like *The Lone Ranger*, where the resolution to virtually every conflict ended in favor of the good guys.

The character of the Lone Ranger, as every Western fan surely knows, originated with Texas Ranger John Reid. The outlaw Cavendish gang ambushed Reid's company of Rangers, killing them all. Or so they thought.

Reid survived and was nursed back to health by Tonto, a Native American. Tonto gave Reid the name Kemo Sabe, meaning faithful friend. When Reid recovered, he and Tonto took revenge on the Cavendish gang. Reid then left both his name, and his life, as he and Tonto devoted themselves to ridding the West of outlaws.

In two extraordinary moves, Reid donned a black mask, traditionally the sign of an outlaw, and his sidekick was a Native American.

Reid, now his company's lone ranger, owned a secret silver mine which provided him with both money and an endless supply of his famed silver bullets.

So it went. The Lone Ranger and Tonto would discover someone had been wronged, or an outlaw was on the loose. They would ride in, and justice prevailed.

Folks they were helping were initially suspicious of the pair. But by the end of the episode they gratefully waved goodbye, asking, "Who was that masked man?"

Clayton Moore, the actor most identified as *The Lone Ranger*, played the character perfectly – straight-faced, perfect grammar, all business. John Hart, who replaced Moore during a contract dispute, was considered less effective.

Jay Silverheels, as Tonto, used his athleticism to excellent effect. (He was a member of the Canadian Lacrosse Hall of Fame.)

The final season was filmed in color even though ABC was broadcasting all its programs in black and white. These 39 color episodes were re-edited into thirteen syndicated "Features," each 77 minutes long titled *Adventures of the Lone Ranger*, with individual sub-titles as to the plot.

Moore and Silverheels also played the leads in a pair of motion pictures: *The Lone Ranger*, and *The Lone Ranger and The Lost City of Gold*.

A third movie, 1981's forgettable *The Legend of the Lone Ranger*, starred Klinton Spilsbury whose dialogue was dubbed by James Keach. Michael Horse was Tonto. The movie's narration ballad, "The Man in the Mask," was performed by country music star Merle Haggard.

The fourth motion picture, 2013's *The Lone Ranger*, was also a poorly received box office failure. The full-blown effort had Johnny Depp as Tonto, Armie Hammer as the Ranger.

Moore died December 28, 1999 at age 86, Silverheels in 1980 at age 67.

The Rifleman

1958 – 1963, ABC, 168 episodes all thirty minutes black & white.

Cast:
Chuck Connors as Lucas McCain
Johnny Crawford as Mark McCain
Paul Fix as Marshal Micah Torrance
Joan Taylor as Milly Scott (1960-1962)
Patricia Blair as Lou Mallory (1962-1963)
Best Ratings: 4th in 1959, 13th in 1960

This series was created by Arnold Laven and the theme song composed by Herschel Burke Gilbert.

Synopsis:
The tall man cocked and fired his rifle so fast the shots could hardly be counted. The shooting over, he twirled the rifle and started reloading. This was the introduction to *The Rifleman*, starring Chuck Connors as Lucas McCain.

One of television's enduring Westerns, *The Rifleman* ran five seasons and has been replayed endlessly in syndication, its 168 episodes airing over and over.

The Rifleman, with gunfights the rule rather than the exception, was pure Western. The list of guest actors who roamed through the series – such as Sammy Davis Jr., Buddy Hackett, Warren Oates, Lee Van Cleef, Michael Ansara – is exceptional.

But another ingredient made this show special. Lucas McCain was a widower raising his son Mark – played by Johnny Crawford – and their relationship was warm and realistic. The friendship between McCain and town marshal Micah Torrance also rang true.

And after two seasons with the elderly Hattie Denton as owner of the general store, love interests came along for Lucas in the form of new store owners Millie Scott, and then Lou Mallory.

Although Arnold Laven is credited with creating *The Rifleman*, the show was initiated by future acclaimed movie director Sam Peckinpah with his *Gunsmoke* script titled "The Sharpshooter."

After being rejected, Peckinpah rewrote the story and sold it to *Dick Powell's Zane Grey Theater*. That became the pilot for *The Rifleman*, and Peckinpah wrote and/or directed five more episodes.

Before filming started, Connors and a production man modified the rifle, a Winchester model 1892 .44-40 carbine. They first installed a large, half-ring lever. In addition to giving the rifle a distinctive look, the ringed lever enabled Connors to easily twirl and cock the gun.

(The series was established as taking place in the early 1880s, but the Winchester model 1892 was not invented until 1892.)

To give McCain an edge in gunfights, a small set screw was placed in the trigger guard. When screwed up, it touched the trigger so that when the lever was cocked and slammed home, the screw tripped the trigger and fired the gun.

These modifications made McCain incredibly fast in a shootout. Being ambidextrous, he was equally effective with either hand.

The Rifleman won critical acclaim for both Connors and Crawford. Connors, a former professional baseball and basketball player, was immensely believable as the strong, agile frontiersman.

Crawford, in 1959, received an Emmy nomination for Best Supporting Actor in a Dramatic Series, won by Dennis Weaver of *Gunsmoke*.

After the fifth season, ABC made plans to expand the show to one hour, in color.

All the principals agreed except Connors. He instead wanted to leave the West to play criminal lawyer John Egan on ABC's *Arrest and Trial*, a 90-minute drama which lasted one season.

Connors and Crawford returned as Lucas and Mark in *The Gambler Returns: The Luck of the Draw*, the often referred to 1991 mini-series starring Kenny Rogers. Crawford had previously appeared in the second mini-series, as a different character.

During Crawford's time on the show he made a splash in the music field with four songs reaching the Billboard Top 40. "Cindy's Birthday" was the highest at number 8.

Connors passed in 1992, at the age of 71, Crawford in 2021, at age 75. Fix died in 1983 at the age of 82.

The Roy Rogers Show

1951 – 1957, NBC, 100 episodes all thirty minutes black & white.

Cast:

Roy Rogers, Dale Evans, Pat Brady

This show was based upon a radio program of the same name. The theme song, "Happy Trails," was written and performed by Roy Rogers and Dale Evans.

Synopsis:

The Roy Rogers Show was an extremely popular "Kiddie Western." While many characters rode horses and carried guns, modern conveniences were also used, such as telephones. Roy's sidekick, Pat Brady, even drove a jeep.

Singing cowboy movie star Roy Rogers and his wife, Dale Evans, were the stars. Roy's horse was Trigger, whom Roy had stuffed and mounted when he died. His dog was named Bullet. Pat's jeep was named Nellybelle. Their adventures were based on the Double R Bar Ranch near Mineral City.

The stories were straightforward and virtually always ended with Roy and friends capturing the bad guys and bringing them in, alive and well.

The show's theme song, "Happy Trails," is a classic, and the popularity which Rogers gained from his movies and this series caused him to be dubbed "King of The Cowboys."

Rogers died in 1998 at the age of 86, and Evans in 2001 at the age of 88. Pat Brady, a World War II veteran of the Battle of the Bulge in Patton's Third Army, died in 1977 at age 57.

The Virginian

1962 – 1971, NBC, 248 episodes all ninety minutes in color.

Cast:

James Drury as the Virginian
Doug McClure as Trampas
Lee J. Cobb as Judge Henry Garth (1962-1966)
Roberta Shore as Betsy (1962-1965)

Randy Boone as Randy (1963-1966)
Clu Gulager as Sheriff Emmett Ryker (1964-1966, 1967-1968)
Gary Clarke as Steve Hill (1962-1964)
Pippa Scott as Molly Wood (1962-1963)
Charles Bickford as John Grainger (1966-1967)
John McIntire as Clay Grainger (1967-1968)
Stewart Granger as Col. Alan MacKenzie (1970-1971)

Best Ratings: 10th in 1967, 14th in 1968, 17th in 1964 and 1969, 22nd in 1965, 25th in 1966.

This program was based upon the 1902 novel by Owen Wister. The theme song for seasons 1 – 8, "The Virginian," was composed by Percy Faith. The theme song for season 9, "Men from Shiloh," was composed by Ennio Morricone.

Synopsis:

The Virginian has the distinction of being the third longest-running Western in network television history, its nine seasons trailing only the 20 of *Gunsmoke* and 14 of *Bonanza*.

Strictly speaking, *The Virginian* had an 8-year run. For the 1970 – '71 season the title was changed to *The Men from Shiloh*, characters were added, and the time period moved forward. But with the series retaining the two primary lead actors and setting, it can be said *The Virginian* lasted nine years and 248 episodes.

It was the first Western to be ninety minutes long.

James Drury in the lead role as *The Virginian* and Doug McClure as Trampas stayed with the show all nine years. Drury's *Virginian* was foreman of the Shiloh Ranch near Medicine Bow, Wyoming. McClure's Trampas was his right-hand man.

Shiloh was owned by four men during the course of the show, the first being Lee J. Cobb as Judge Henry Garth.

When Cobb left during season four, Judge Garth was written out by having him become governor of Wyoming, John Dehner as Morgan Starr became the temporary ranch manager.

Owners during the remainder of the show were played by Charles Bickford, John McIntire and Stewart Granger.

Several supporting actors had roles at different times, three being Clu Gulager as Sheriff Emmett Ryker, Gary Clarke as Steve Hill, and Roberta Shore as Betsy.

Stories revolved around the residents of Shiloh and their adventures, usually involving a wide range of guest stars.

The Virginian novel was made into two theatrical motion pictures, in 1929 with Gary Cooper and Walter Huston, and 1946 with Joel McCrea. A television movie was made in 2000 starring Bill Pullman and Diane Lane, with Dennis Weaver in a small role.

Although their characters weren't mentioned by name, Drury and McClure had parts in, yes, Kenny Rogers's 1991 *The Gambler Returns: The Luck of the Draw*. They played a couple of rodeo cowboys who no longer worked for, "That sorry old outfit," as McClure's character put it.

Drury died in 2020 at the age of 85. McClure passed at age 59, in 1995, Cobb at age 64, in 1976.

The thirty minute, black and white *Virginian* pilot, different in tone and also starring Drury, aired on the 1958 NBC summer series, *Decision*.

Wagon Train

1957 – 1962 NBC, 1962 – 1965 ABC, 253 episodes: 221 one hour, 32 ninety minutes black & white and color.

Cast:
Ward Bond as Major Seth Adams (1957-1961)
Robert Horton as Flint McCullough (1957-1962)
John McIntire as Christopher Hale (1961-1965)
Robert Fuller as Cooper Smith (1963-1965)
Frank McGrath as Charlie Wooster
Terry Wilson as Bill Hawks

Best Ratings: 1st in 1962, 2nd in 1959, 1960, and 1961, 23rd in 1958, 25th in 1963.

Wagon Train was inspired by the John Ford motion picture, *Wagon Master*. The show had three theme songs:
Season 1 "Wagon Train," was written by Henri Rene and Bob Russell.
Season 2 "Roll Along Wagon Train," was written by Sammy Fain and Jack Brooks, and performed by Johnny O'Neill.
Seasons 3 – 8, "Wagons Ho," was written by Jerome Moross.

Synopsis:
For eight years, 1957 to 1965, *Wagon Train* rumbled West, meeting characters and having adventures of all types along the way.

Wagon Train was enormously popular for several years. In 1962, the show became one of only three Westerns to finish a season rated number one, the others being *Gunsmoke* and *Bonanza*. It had earlier finished second for three consecutive years.

The reasons for *Wagon Train's* success were several. Ward Bond and Robert Horton were excellent in the lead roles as wagon master, Major Seth Adams, and his scout, Flint McCullough. Bond's Adams was a Civil War veteran, hence the title "Major."

Terry Wilson was assistant wagon master and lead driver Bill Hawks, and Frank McGrath was grizzled, fast talking cook, Charlie Wooster.

The show's episodes were primarily straight Western dramas, with numerous guest stars in featured roles.

After the show's fourth season – its third straight at number two – Ward Bond died at the age of 57.

John McIntire was brought in to play new wagon master Christopher Hale. McIntire proved to be as effective as Bond, and in its fifth season he and Horton led *Wagon Train* to the number one spot on television.

But then Horton announced he was leaving the series, and the show changed networks, from NBC to ABC. Robert Fuller came in to play new scout, Cooper Smith. Fuller was a Western veteran, having earlier co-starred in *Laramie*.

The changes proved difficult, and *Wagon Train* fell from first to 25th.

In an effort to revive the fallen giant, ABC changed the program to a full color, 90-minute format. Ratings failed to improve, and for the 1964-'65 season *Wagon Train* returned to one hour. But the show had run its course, and after season eight, was cancelled.

Of the lead actors, Horton died in 2016 at age 91, McIntire in 1991 at age 83, McGrath in 1967 at age 64, and Wilson in 1999 at age 75.

Wagon Train, with its brilliant ratings from 1959 until 1962, and with its 253 episodes being third among all network television Westerns, stakes a rightful claim as being one of the greats.

A Man Called Shenandoah to *Zorro*

~ ~

The Remainder of Television Westerns

A Man Called Shenandoah

1965 – 1966, ABC, 34 episodes all thirty minutes black & white.

Cast:

Robert Horton as Shenandoah

This series was created by E. Jack Neuman. The theme song was the traditional American folk melody, "Oh Shenandoah," with new lyrics written and performed by Robert Horton.

Synopsis:

In 1962 Robert Horton, said to be tired of Westerns, left *Wagon Train,* the number one rated show on television. Three years later he turned up on this short-lived series. Horton's character was an amnesia victim trying to learn his past.

Horton, who had performed in musical theater, released the album, *The Man Called Shenandoah* in 1965 and the show's theme song, "Oh Shenandoah," was a single.

Action in the Afternoon

1953 – 1954, CBS (The show aired for one calendar year.), thirty minutes black and white.

Cast:

Jack Valentine as the Singing Cowboy
Mary Watts as Red Cotton
Barry Cassell as Ace Bandcroft
Blake Ritter, Narrator

This show was created by Charles Vanda. The opening theme, "Billy the Kid," was composed by Aaron Copland.

Synopsis:

Action in the Afternoon is thought to be the only completely live Western to air on a daily basis. The show was filmed in Philadelphia, and aired five afternoons a week.

The outside set was a dirt-covered parking lot with false-front buildings. A totem pole disguised a telephone pole.

Outdoor scenes were shot live each day, regardless of the weather. In addition to contending with the noise of automobiles and airplanes, wind occasional blew down the building fronts.

Horses sometimes caused problems. A hanging scene nearly resulted in a real hanging when a horse spooked. In another show, two actors jumped on horses to give chase. One horse took off and the other didn't move, to which the quick-thinking actor yelled, "I'll catch up to you later!"

Valentine and the Ferguson Trio would break into song at a moment's notice to fill time, for a multitude of reasons.

Alias Smith & Jones

1971 – 1973, ABC, 50 episodes one hour long, in color.

Cast:

Ben Murphy as Jedediah "Kid" Curry
Pete Duel (first 33 episodes) as Hannibal Heyes.
Roger Davis as Hannibal Hayes

This series was created by Glen Larson. The theme song was composed by Billy Goldenberg.

Synopsis:

This entertaining, lighthearted series was similar in style to the popular motion picture, *Butch Cassidy and the Sundance Kid*. With executive producer Roy Huggins writing most of the episodes, it also resembled his *Maverick*.

Curry and Heyes – alias Thaddeus Jones and Joshua Smith – were successful outlaws who had managed to never shoot anyone. When the two decided to go straight, they contacted the governor and asked for amnesty.

The governor agreed, providing the two could prove they deserved amnesty by staying out of trouble until the time was politically correct. No one else knew of this conditional amnesty, not bounty hunters, lawmen, nor former gang members.

This series featured guest appearances by a host of veteran Western actors, including Pernell Roberts, Paul Fix, Jack Elam, Neville Brand, James Drury, John Russell, Lee Majors, and Walter Brennan in a recurring role.

Following the suicide of Peter Duel at the age of 31 on New Year's Eve, 1971, Roger Davis was cast as Hannibal Heyes. Davis had provided voiceover narration during opening credits, and had appeared in one episode.

The ninety-minute pilot aired three weeks before the series began.

Annie Oakley

1954 – 1957, Syndicated, 80 episodes all thirty minutes black & white.

Cast:

Gail Davis as Annie Oakley
Brad Johnson as Deputy Sheriff Lofty Craig
Jimmy Hawkins as Tagg Oakley

The theme song for this program was composed by Erma Levin.

Synopsis:

This kiddie Western had Annie Oakley as the prettiest girl and best shot in Diablo County, Arizona.

Annie and her brother, Tagg, were orphans who lived with their uncle, the sheriff. He was too busy to be around much, so Deputy Lofty Craig kept an eye on them.

Gail Davis died at the age of 71, in 1997.

Barbary Coast

1975 – 1976, ABC, 13 episodes all one-hour color.

Cast:

William Shatner as Jeff Cable
Doug McClure as Cash Conover
This program was created by Douglas Heyes.

Synopsis:

San Francisco's notorious Barbary Coast was the setting for this short-lived show which starred *Star Trek's* William Shatner and *The Virginian's* Doug McClure.

Borrowing from *The Wild Wild West*, *Barbary Coast* had Shatner's character as a government agent working undercover in a variety of disguises.

McClure's Conover, owner of the Golden Gate Casino, provided assistance.

Barbary Coast also used elements from *Mission Impossible*, even hiring several of their writers.

Bat Masterson

1958 – 1961, NBC, 108 episodes all thirty minutes black & white.

Cast:

Gene Barry as Bat Masterson

This program was based upon Masterson's biography which was written by Richard O'Connor. The theme song was composed by Havens Wray with lyrics by Bart Corwin. The song was performed by Bill Lee.

Synopsis:

Bat Masterson was an Old West lawman who was friends with Wyatt Earp, wore tailored clothes, a derby hat, carried a gold-tipped cane, and packed a custom-made pistol.

As portrayed by Gene Barry, television's "Bat" was all the above, and was one of the television West's more unique characters.

Barry reprised the character twice, on the CBS series, *Paradise*, in 1990, and a year later on *The Gambler Returns: The Luck of the Draw*.

Barry died in 2009, at the age of 90.

Branded

1965 – 1966 NBC, 48 episodes all thirty minutes (13 black and white, 35 color).

Cast:

Chuck Connors as Jason McCord

This series was created by Larry Cohen. The theme song was composed by Dominic Frontiere with lyrics by Alan Alch. The performer is not credited.

Synopsis:

As the song declares, all but one man died in the Battle of Bitter Creek, Wyoming – U.S. Army Captain Jason McCord. Did he survive because he ran and hid, as the Army thinks, or because he was knocked unconscious and thought dead, which McCord believes?

No one knew for sure. So, the Army stripped McCord of his rank, branded him a coward, and kicked him out of the service. He then roamed the West, trying to find an eyewitness to the battle and dealing with insults when others discovered the coward, Jason McCord, was in town.

Chuck Connors, two years removed from Lucas McCain on *The Rifleman*, was in fine form as McCord. He carried a broken sword compliments of the Army, and could twirl and throw it with accuracy.

Branded was one show which needed an ending. Although a Native American survivor to the battle apparently confirmed McCord's innocence, no one said for sure.

Airing immediately before the top-rated *Bonanza*, *Branded* was 14th in the ratings in 1965.

Brave Eagle

1955 – 1956, CBS, 39 episodes all thirty minutes black & white.

Cast:

Keith Larsen as Brave Eagle
Keena Nomkeena as Keena
Kim Winono as Morning Star

Synopsis:

This series was the first to feature a Native American primary character, and told stories from the Native American point of view.

In addition to dealing with other tribes and white men, Cheyenne chief Brave Eagle raised his foster son Keena, and romanced Morning Star.

Larsen, who later played in *Northwest Passage*, died in 2006 at age 82.

Broken Arrow

1956 – 1958, ABC, 72 episodes all thirty minutes black & white.

Cast:

Michael Ansara as Cochise
John Lupton as Tom Jeffords

Broken Arrow was based upon Elliott Arnold's book, *Blood Brother*, and a movie of the same name starring James Stewart and Jeff Chandler. The theme song was composed by Stanley Wilson, Paul Sawtell, and Ned Washington.

Synopsis:

The show was somewhat distinctive for its era – a Western in which Whites and Native Americans tried to be friends.

Indian Agent Tom Jeffords, played by John Lupton, was blood brother to Cochise, played by Michael Ansara. Together they fought dishonest white men and renegades from the Chiricahua Reservation.

Ansara died in 2013, at age 91, Lupton in 1993, at 65.

Boots and Saddles

1956 – 1957, NBC, 39 episodes, thirty minutes black & white.

Cast:

John Pickard as Capt. Shank Adams
Michael Hinn as Scout

This series was created by Robert Cinader. The theme song was composed by Fred Steiner.

Synopsis:

Boots and Saddles was one of the first shows to use actual locations, in Kanab, Utah. It featured the U.S. Calvary of 1870's Arizona as they fought outlaws and Geronimo.

Pickard died at age 80, in 1993, Hinn at age 75, in 1988.

Bronco

1958 – 1962, ABC, 69 episodes, all one-hour black & white.

Cast:
Ty Hardin as Bronco Layne

The theme song for this program was composed by Mark David and Jay Livingston, with lyrics by Paul Sawtell.

Synopsis:
Bronco, along with *Sugarfoot*, was created when production of *Cheyenne* began to slow. The three shows alternated in the same time slot.

Stories did not follow any chronological order. One episode might find Bronco involved with Billy the Kid in 1878, and in the next meet Cole Younger in 1863.

Hardin died in 2017, at the age of 87.

Buckskin

1958 – 1959, NBC, 39 episodes, all thirty minutes black & white.

Cast:
Tommy Nolan as Jody O'Connell
Sallie Brophy as Annie O'Connell
Michael Road as Marshal Tom Sellers

This series was created by Harold Swanton. The theme song was composed by Stanley Morton and Mort Green.

Synopsis:
This series showed Western life in Buckskin, Montana, through the eyes of ten-year-old Jody O'Connell, who narrated each episode while playing a harmonica on a corral fence.

Jody's mother, Annie, operated the Buckskin boarding house. The town marshal was Tom Sellers.

Buckskin suffered from not having a fixed time slot.

Brophy died at age 78, in 2007; Road in 2013, at age 95.

Buffalo Bill Jr.

1955 – 1956, CBS, 52 episodes all thirty minutes black & white.

Cast:
Dick Jones as Buffalo Bill Jr.
The theme song was composed by Carl Cotner.

Synopsis:
Trick rider and roper Dick Jones played the fictional son of Old West legend Buffalo Bill, fighting for justice in Wileyville, Texas.
    Jones died at age 87, in 2014.

Casey Jones

1957 – 1958, Syndicated, 32 episodes all thirty minutes black & white.

Cast:
Alan Hale Jr. as Casey Jones
Bobby Clark as Casey Jr.
Dub Taylor as Wally Sims

    This series was based upon Casey Jones, a railroader who was killed in a train wreck at age 37, in 1900. The theme song is derived from "The Ballad of Casey Jones;" the writer of the new lyrics is not credited.

Synopsis:
    Before Alan Hale Jr. became everlastingly entrenched as the Skipper on *Gilligan's Island*, he was Casey Jones in this entertaining, well-made series.
    Trains in the Old West, of course, were subject to a myriad of problems beyond holdups, which gave Casey plenty to do.
    The rapport between the likeable Hale and young Bobby Clark as Casey Jr. enriched the show, as did Dub Taylor's portrayal of the fireman, Sims.
    Although being a light-hearted series, *Casey Jones* occasionally featured mature elements which placed it in-between the Kiddies and Adult categories.
    Alan Hale Jr. died in 1990 at the age of 68, Dub Taylor in 1994 at age 87.

Cimarron City

1958 – 1959, NBC, 16 episodes all one-hour black & white.

Cast:

George Montgomery as Matthew Rockford
Audrey Totter as Beth Purcell
John Smith as Lane Temple
Dan Blocker as Tiny Budinger

The theme song for this program was composed by Frederick Herbert and Stanley Wilson.

Synopsis:

Cimarron City is noteworthy because the star, George Montgomery, provided narration, and featured Dan Blocker immediately before he landed the role of *Bonanza's* Hoss Cartwright. Smith was later to co-star in *Laramie*.

Montgomery played town leader Matthew Rockford. He, boarding house owner Beth Purcell, sheriff Lane Temple, and good citizen Tiny Budinger did everything within their power to see that boom town Cimarron City become the capital of the soon-to-be state comprising the Oklahoma Territory.

Montgomery died at age 84, in 2000; Totter age 95, in 2013.

Cimarron Strip

1967 – 1968, CBS, 23 episodes all ninety-minute color.

Cast:

Stuart Whitman as U.S. Marshal Jim Crown

This series was created by Christopher Knopf. The theme song was composed by Maurice Jarre.

Synopsis:

Cimarron Strip was CBS's entry in the ninety-minute TV Western sweepstakes which was started, and dominated, by NBC's *The Virginian*.

Stories centered around U.S. Marshal Jim Crown's efforts in bringing law and order to the Cimarron Strip, later to become the Oklahoma Panhandle.

Whitman died in 2020, at age 92.

Colt .45

1957 – 1960, ABC, 67 episodes all thirty minutes black & white

Cast:

Wayde Preston as Christopher Colt
Donald May as Sam Colt, Jr.

This show was developed by Roy Huggins and based upon a film of the same name starring Randolph Scott. The theme song was composed by Mack Davis and Jerry Livingston. It was performed by Hal Hooper.

Synopsis:

Christopher Colt, son of Samuel Colt – who invented the Colt .45 revolver – traveled the West in the guise of a gun salesman.

He was actually a government undercover agent, seeking outlaws and the like. This gave him plenty of opportunity to use his dad's pistols, which he was an ace with. Colt encountered several characters based upon historical figures.

When difficulties developed between Preston and Warner Brothers (a recurring theme with the studio and their stars), Donald May was brought in to play Colt's cousin, Sam Colt, Jr., who had the same job. Preston eventually returned, as a co-star.

Preston died in 1992 age 62.

Cowboy G-Men

1952 – 1953, Syndicated, 39 thirty-minute episodes (sources indicate the show was filmed in color, but aired in black & white).

Cast:

Russell Hayden as Pat Gallagher
Jackie Coogan as Stoney Crockett

This program was based upon a story by Henry Donovan.

Synopsis:

Fans of *The Addams Family* might enjoy watching this show, which co-starred "Uncle Fester" himself, Jackie Coogan, as Stoney Crockett.

Aimed for the youngsters, *Cowboy G-Men* featured "Cowboy" government agents Pat Gallagher and Stoney Crockett – the "G-Men," – fighting desperados.

Hayden died at age 68, in 1981; Coogan age 69, in 1984.

Cowboys & Injuns

1950, ABC, 13 episodes all thirty minutes black & white.
Hosted by Rex Bell.

Synopsis:

This children's show gave demonstrations of real cowboys and Native American customs, and stories. In addition to being filmed indoors, it also went on location to an outdoor corral and a Native American village.

Cowboy Theater

1957, NBC, 18 black & white episodes: four thirty minutes, fourteen one hour.
Hosted by Monty Hall.

Synopsis:

Cowboy Theater was an anthology series using re-edited Columbia Pictures movies from the 1930's and 1940's.

Narrator Monty Hall later gained more fame hosting *Let's Make a Deal.*

Custer

1967, ABC, 17 one-hour episodes, all in color. The show is also known as, *The Legend of Custer.*

Cast:
    Wayne Maunder as Lt. Col. George A. Custer
    Slim Pickens as Joe Milner

Synopsis:
After being demoted from Major General to Lt. Colonel, and before being annihilated at the Battle of Little Big Horn, George Armstrong Custer commanded the 7th Cavalry Regiment at Fort Hays, Kansas.

    Aided by Pickens' Joe Milner, Custer shaped the 7th into an effective fighting outfit.

    Maunder died in 2018, at age 80. Pickens, a noted character actor on television and film, died in 1983, at age 64.

Destry

1964, ABC, 13 episodes, all one-hour black & white.

Cast:
    John Gavin as Harrison Destry

    This series was based on the Max Brand novel, *Destry Rides Again*. The character of Tom Destry was featured in a Broadway musical which starred Andy Griffith, and in several movies. The theme song was composed by Randy Sparks and performed by The Ledbetters.

Synopsis:
This series featured Tom's son, Harrison Destry, as a former lawman who had been wrongly convicted of a crime. After his release from prison, Harrison looked for those who had framed him. Humor found its way into many situations.

    Series star, John Gavin, was appointed U.S. Ambassador to Mexico from 1981 until 1986. He had been born Juan Vincent Apablasa Jr., and died at age 86, in 2018.

Dirty Sally

1974, CBS, 14 episodes, all thirty minutes color.
This show was created by Jack Miller.

Cast:

Jeanette Nolan as Sally Fergus
Dack Rambo as Cyrus Pike

Synopsis:

The character of *Dirty Sally* appeared in the *Gunsmoke* two-part episode "Pike" (retitled "Dirty Sally" in syndication) and a sequel, "One for the Road."

The character was so popular CBS awarded Nolan her own *Dirty Sally* series in which she was traveling to California with a former gunslinger, Rambo's Pike. Her popularity, however, failed to carry over into this show.

Nolan died in 1998 at the age of 86, Rambo in 1994 at age 52.

Dundee and the Culhane

1967, CBS, 13 episodes, all one-hour color.

Cast:

John Mills as Dundee
Sean Garrison as Culhan

This series was created by Sam Rolfe and the theme song composed by David Rose.

Synopsis:

Dundee was a British attorney with offices in Sausalito, across the bay from San Francisco. Culhane (who was referred to as The Culhane) was his handsome, fast drawing apprentice lawyer. The two traveled the Old West, helping their clients.

Mills died in 2005, at the age of 97, Garrison in 2018 at age of 80.

Dusty's Trail

1973 – 1974, Syndicated, 26 episodes all thirty minutes color.

Cast:

Bob Denver as Dusty
Forrest Tucker as Callahan

This series was created by Sherwood Schwartz and the theme composed by Frank De Vol and Jack Pielst.

Synopsis:

This show was simply Schwartz placing his *Gilligan's Island* crew lost in the Old West. Rather than being named Gilligan, Denver was Dusty, scout for Tucker's wagon master Callahan.

Those two, along with five travelers, become separated from their wagon train going to California. Other than names, the seven were identical to the island castaways.

In 1976, four episodes of the series were edited into the theatrical film, *The Wackiest Wagon Train in the West*.

Denver died in 2005, at age 70.

F Troop

1965 – 1967, ABC, 65 episodes (34 black & white, 31 color).

Cast:

Ken Berry as Capt. William Parmenter
Forrest Tucker as Sgt. Morgan O'Rourke
Larry Storch as Cpl. Randolph Agarn

This series was created by Seaman Jacobs, Ed James, and Jim Barnett. The theme song was composed and written by Irving Taylor and William Lava. The performers were not credited.

Synopsis:

F Troop was a Western played for laughs. Stationed at Fort Courage after the Civil War, F Troop was under the command of Capt. William Parmenter.

During the war he had thrown his arm forward during a sneeze, causing his men to charge and snatch victory from certain defeat. Parmenter was proclaimed a hero, given a medal, and given his own fort.

The bumbling captain, played by Ken Berry, was usually lost as to the events around him.

Forrest Tucker's Sgt. Morgan O'Rourke kept the troop going through successful trading with the Hekawi Indians. Chief Wild Eagle led the Hekawis, who wanted to be known as lovers, not fighters.

Cpl. Randolph Agarn was O'Rourke's right-hand man, and Crazy Cat was Wild Eagle's second banana.

Fast shooting, hard riding cowgirl Wrangler Jane was out to marry Parmenter, and would go to almost any extreme to try and nab him.

Other regulars in Fort Courage included a blind lookout, a tone-deaf bugler, and a private who spoke German.

Guest stars included Phil Harris as 147-year-old Flaming Arrow, Don Rickles as Bald Eagle, Milton Berle as Indian detective Wise Owl, Paul Lynde as singing Mountie Sgt. Ramseden, and Henry Gibson as unlucky calvary trooper Wrongo Starr.

Berry died in 2018, at the age of 85. Tucker died in 1986, at age 67.

Frontier

1955 – 1956, NBC, 31 episodes all thirty minutes black & white.

This series was created by Morton Fine and David Friedkin, and narrated by Walter Coy.

Synopsis:

This anthology series dealt with the hazards which settlers encountered making their way West. Similar in style to *Death Valley Days*, *Frontier* was nominated for an Emmy its one season.

Narrator Walter Coy acted in some of the episodes. He died in 1974, at the age of 65.

Frontier Circus

1961 – 1962, CBS, 26 episodes all one-hour black & white.

Cast:

Chill Wills as Col. Casey Thompson
John Derek as Ben Travis
Richard Jaeckel as Tony Gentry

Synopsis:

The T&T Circus traveled throughout the Old West, giving performances in towns they came to.

Col. Casey Thompson was the manager, Ben Travis the straw boss, and Tony Gentry the advance man. John Derek, who played Travis, gained more fame a couple of decades later as the husband of his fourth wife, actress Bo Derek.

Wills died at age 76 in 1978, Derek age 71 in 1998, and Jaeckel age 70, in 1997.

Frontier Doctor

1956 – 1957, Syndicated, 39 episodes all thirty minutes black & white. This show was also known as *Unarmed* and *Man of the West*.

Cast:

Rex Allen as Dr. Bill Baxter
Based upon an idea by Rex Allen.

Synopsis:

In this series country and western singer and minor movie star Rex Allen played a doctor in the Arizona Territory.

With doctors being far between and medicine relatively scarce, he stayed busy. The doctor did not carry a gun, but did not hesitate to borrow one, if needed.

Frontier Justice

1958 – 1961, CBS, 34 episodes all thirty minutes black & white.
Hosts: Lew Ayres, Melvyn Douglas, Ralph Bellamy

Synopsis:

Frontier Justice was reruns of *Dick Powell's Zane Grey Theater* which CBS aired for three summers. The only difference was replacing host Dick Powell with Lew Ayres, Melvyn Douglas, and Ralph Bellamy, who served one summer each.

Gunslinger

1961, CBS, 12 episodes all one-hour black & white.

Cast:
Tony Young as Cord

Synopsis:
Cord was a gunslinger with no last name, working undercover for Fort Scott, New Mexico's Captain Zachary Wingate.
Tony Young died in 2002, at age 64.

Here Comes the Brides

1968 – 1970, ABC, 52 episodes, all one-hour color.

Cast:
Robert Brown as Jason Bolt
Bobby Sherman as Jeremy Bolt
David Soul as Joshua Bolt
Mark Leonard as Aaron Stempel
Joan Blondell as Lottie Hatfield

This show was inspired by the motion picture *Seven Brides for Seven Brothers*, and by the real-life Asa Mercer's Girls Project.

The song, *Seattle*, served as the theme song. It was composed by Hugo Montenegro, with lyrics by Jack Keller and Ernie Shelton. Perry Como's release was a top 40 hit. Show co-star Bobby Sherman also recorded the song, but it was never released as a single.

Synopsis:
Although *Here Comes the Brides* was set in the West after the Civil War, the show might also be called a Romantic Comedy.

Lonely lumberjacks in Seattle were ready to return East for female companionship. The Bolt brothers, managers of the local sawmill, instead traveled to Massachusetts and recruited one hundred women to come with them to Bridal Veil Mountain.

Sawmill owner Aaron Stempel financed the affair. Local saloon owner Lottie Hatfield provided a mother figure for the ladies.

Stories focused on relationships, social issues, even ecology. Gunplay was absent, with fistfights being comedic.

Bobby Sherman, who played a Bolt, had a successful singing career. In an interesting turn, his character of Jeremy stuttered. David Soul – another Bolt – later received more acclaim as Hutch in the series *Starsky and Hutch*.

Mark Leonard died in 1996 at age 72, Joan Blondell in 1979 at age 73.

Hondo

1967, ABC, 15 episodes all one-hour color.

Cast:

Ralph Taeger as Hondo Lane

Hondo was developed by Andrew Fenady. The show was based upon the novel by Louis L'Amour and the 1953 John Wayne movie, both of the same name. The theme song was composed by Richard Markowitz.

Synopsis:

Hondo Lane and his dog, Sam, troubleshoot for the Army in 1870's Arizona Territory.

Hondo had been a captain in the Confederate Army, moved West and married a Native American girl who was killed in an Army attack. Hondo then tried to find peaceful solutions to problems faced by both the white men and his blood brothers.

Ralph Taeger died in 2015, at age 78.

Hopalong Cassidy

1951 – 1952, Syndicated, 52 episodes all thirty minutes black & white.

Cast:

William Boyd as Hopalong Cassidy
Edgar Buchanan as Red Conner

This television show, along with a radio program and more than sixty movies, was based upon books and short stories written by Clarence Mulford which featured Hopalong Cassidy.

Synopsis:

In the late 1940's, television stations began airing edited versions of the *Hopalong Cassidy* movies which had been produced in the 1930's and 1940's.

They proved popular with younger viewers, so William Boyd reprised the role in an all-new, made-for-television thirty-minute weekly series which was rated 9th in 1951.

The show was a Kiddie Western in every way. "Hoppy" wore a perfectly pressed black outfit, and his sidekick was Red Conners, played by Edgar Buchanan of future *Petticoat Junction* fame.

Boyd's portrayal of "Hoppy" differed from Mulford's writing, in which the character drank liquor, smoked, swore, and gained his first name because he limped. Boyd cleaned him up, completely.

Boyd died in 1972, at age 77. Buchanan died at age 76, in 1979.

Hotel De Pardee

1959 – 1960, CBS, 33 episodes all thirty-minute black & white.

Cast:

Earl Holliman as Sundance
The theme song for this program was composed by Dimitri Tiomkin.

Synopsis:

Released from prison, Sundance returned to Georgetown, Colorado, where he had killed a man seventeen years earlier. He became the town's peacemaker, along with becoming co-owner of the fancy Hotel De Paree. His partner was the lovely French lady Annette, whose equally lovely niece was Monique.

In another TV West gimmick, Sundance wore polished, mirrored silver discs in the hatband of his black Stetson. Adversaries were therefore temporarily blinded, giving Sundance the edge in gunfights.

How the West Was Won

1976 – 1979, ABC, color. This program started as *The Macahans*, a 1976 made-for-television movie. The story resumed in the 1977 mini-series, *How the West was Won*, and continued with that title as a somewhat irregular series in 1978 and 1979.

Cast:

James Arness as Zeb Macahan
Bruce Boxleitner as Luke Macahan
William Kirby Cullen as Josh Macahan
Fionnula Flanagan as Molly Culhan

This program was inspired by a 1962 film of the same name. The theme song was composed by Jerrold Immel.

Synopsis:

One year after turning in his marshal's badge, James Arness was back on television as rugged mountain man Zeb Macahan, who returned home to Virginia after a decade in the Dakota Territory.

With the Civil War looming Zeb headed West again, this time with his brother Timothy (Richard Kiley) and family.

The elder Macahan parents refused to leave. After several months Timothy came back for them, with eldest son Luke later following.

The storylines followed Luke's adventures as a wanted man and gunfighter, and Zeb as he led the clan through the raw territory. The Macahans eventually settled in the Tetons.

Gunsmoke producer John Mantley served as executive producer of *How the West Was Won*. The show was greatly enhanced by spectacular location filming in Utah, Colorado, Arizona, and California.

Iron Horse

1966 – 1968, ABC, 47 episodes all one-hour, color.

Cast:

Dale Robertson as Ben Calhoun

This series was created by James Goldstone and Stephen Kandel. The theme song was composed by Dominic Frontiere.

Synopsis:

Dale Robertson, veteran Western actor from *Tales of Wells Fargo*, returned to the TV West with *Iron Horse*. Robertson's Ben Calhoun had won the decrepit railroad line, *Buffalo Pass, Scalplock, and Defiance* in a poker game.

Calhoun was determined to improve and expand the line no matter what Old West obstacles got in his way.

The television movie, *Scalplock*, served as the show's pilot.

Jefferson Drum

1958 – 1959, NBC 26 episodes all thirty minutes black & white.
The show was also known as *The Pen & the Quill*.

Cast:

Jeff Richards as Jefferson Drum
Eugene Martin as Joey Drum
Robert Stevenson as Big Ed

Synopsis:

Newspaper editor Jefferson Drum tried to bring order to the mining town of Jubilee.

When his pen didn't work, he took up the gun, assisted by bartender Big Ed.

A widower, Drum was also raising son Joey.

Hal Smith, later to be Otis Campbell on *The Andy Griffith Show*, made several appearances as townsman Hickey. The creator of *Star Trek*, Gene Roddenberry, was a writer for the series.

Richards, a veteran of World War II and a minor league baseball player, died in 1969 at age 64. Stevenson died in 1975 at age 59. Smith passed at age 77, in 1994.

Johnny Ringo

1959 – 1960, CBS 38 episodes, all thirty minutes black & white.

Cast:

Don Durant as Johnny Ringo
Karen Sharpe as Laura Thomas

Mark Goddard as Cully

This series was created by Aaron Spelling, the theme song composed by Roy Schrager and Herschel Burke Gilbert.

Synopsis:

Johnny Ringo was the sheriff of Velardi, Arizona. A former gunslinger, he used his talent for the cause of justice. Rather than a traditional pistol, Ringo used a LeMat. Introduced during the Civil War, the LeMat was a pistol with an auxiliary shotgun barrel.

Laura Thomas was Johnny's love interest. Mark Goddard, who played Cully the deputy, was to become *Lost in Space* four years later.

The pilot episode, "Man Alone," aired on *Dick Powell's Zane Grey Theater*. Ringo was a real-life gunfighter turned lawman in the 1880's.

Durant died at age 72, in 2005.

Kung Fu

1972 – 1975, ABC, 63 episodes all one-hour color.

Cast:

David Carradine as Kwai Chang Caine
Radames Pera as young Caine
Keye Luke as Maser Po
Philip Ahn as Master Kan

This series was created by Ed Spielman, Jerry Thorpe, and Herman Miller.

Synopsis:

Cain, the son of Chinese and American parents, was raised in a Chinese orphanage. He was a Buddhist monk and a master of the Chinese martial art of kung fu.

After being forced to kill a member of the Chinese royal family, he fled to the American Old West. In addition to dealing with prejudice, Caine had to keep a step ahead of bounty hunters as he roamed the West, looking for his half-brother.

Caine helped those in need and dealt with fists, guns, and knives the same way – with kung fu, usually in slow motion. Flashbacks were frequent, depicting young Caine's education by Masters Po and Kan.

Caine spoke little; when he did it was often to share a cryptic phrase taught to him by his masters.

Carradine was chosen for the role over Bruce Lee, an actual martial arts expert who became a short-lived film star. The pilot was aired on *ABC Movie of the Week.*

Carradine returned in a pair of made-for-television movie sequels, *Kung Fu: The Movie,* and *Kung Fu: The Next Generation,* and in the contemporary series, *Kung Fu: The Legend Continues.*

He also made an appearance in the *Luck of the Draw* mini-series with Kenny Rogers.

Carradine died in 2009, at age 72. Keye Luke died in 1991 at age 86, Philip Ahn passed in 1978 at age 72.

Lancer

1968 – 1970, CBS, 51 episodes all one-hour color.

Cast:

James Stacy as Johnny Lancer
Wayne Maunder as Scott Lancer
Andrew Duggan as Murdock Lancer
Elizabeth Baur as Teresa O'Brien
Paul Brinegar as Jelly Hoskins

This series was created by Samuel A. Peeples. The theme song was composed by Jerome Moross.

Synopsis:

Murdock Lancer operated a large horse and sheep ranch in the 1870's California San Joaquin Valley. He was assisted by Teresa O'Brien, the daughter of Lancer's dead foreman.

Land pirates were a major problem, so Murdock brought in his two adult sons to help. Born of different mothers, they had not seen each other since they were boys. Johnny was a drifter and gunfighter, and Scott was a college graduate living in Boston.

The sons helped keep the ranch intact, each with an eye for Teresa.

Paul Brinegar, not long removed from *Rawhide,* soon provided more help as Jelly Hoskins.

Duggan died at age 64 in 1988, Stacy at age 79 in 2016, Maunder at age 80 in 2018, Baur at age 69 in 2017.

Laramie

1959 – 1963 NBC, 124 one-hour episodes, 64 black & white and 60 color.

Cast:

John Smith as Slim Sherman
Robert Fuller as Jess Harper

The theme song for this program was composed by Cyril Mockridge. The lyrics – which were never used – were written by Bill Olafson.

Synopsis:

Laramie enjoyed a four-year, 124-episode run on NBC. Slim Sherman and his partner, Jess Harper, operated a combination ranch/relay station near Laramie, Wyoming. The stage allowed numerous outlaws to come by for Slim and Jess to deal with.

Bobby Crawford, Jr., the older brother of *The Rifleman's* Johnny Crawford, played Slim's brother, Andy, for two seasons. The first season had singer Hoagy Carmichael as Jonesy. Spring Byington was cook and housekeeper Daisy Cooper the last two years.

Although *Laramie* never broke the ratings top twenty-five, the program allowed Robert Fuller to get established as a Western actor – the better to go on to *Wagon Train*.

John Smith died at age 63, in 1995.

Laredo

1965 – 1967, NBC, 56 episodes all one-hour color.

Cast:

Neville Brand as Reese Bennett
Peter Brown as Chad Cooper
William Smith as Joe Riley
Philip Carey as Capt. Edward Parmalee
Robert Wolders as Erik Hunter (1966-1967)

Laredo was created by Richard Irving. The theme song was composed by Russel Garcia.

Synopsis:

Laredo was a Western with plenty of humor.

Laredo, Texas was the home base for the post-civil war Texas Rangers, Company B, under the command of Captain Edward Parmalee. His Rangers were effective in spite of lots of horseplay, especially from Neville Brand.

Cast opposite his usually tough character, Brand's Reese Bennett was an aging gunslinger who joined the Rangers for protection against lawmen who might still be after him.

William Smith's Joe Riley joined for the same reason. Peter Brown – formally the *Lawman's* deputy – played Chad Cooper. He joined the Rangers to hunt American gunrunners who sold weapons to Mexican outlaws, who then killed most of Cooper's Civil War Border Patrol.

Robert Wolders' character of Erik Hunter was added to the cast for the second season.

Laredo's pilot was the episode "We've Lost a Train," on *The Virginian*. It was later released as the motion picture, *Backtrack*.

And three episodes from the first season were edited into a 1968 movie, *Three Guns for Texas*.

Brand – a highly decorated combat soldier in World War II – died in 1992 at age 71, Brown in 2016 at age 80, Carey in 2009 at age 87, Wolders in 2018 at age 81.

Lash of the West

1953, ABC, fifteen minutes black & white.
   Host: Lash LaRue

Synopsis:

Popular 1940's cowboy movie star Lash LaRue hosted this program, which used edited scenes from his movies.

LaRue, known for his prowess with a bullwhip, died in 1996, at age 78.

Law of the Plainsman

1959 – 1960 NBC, 30 episodes all thirty minutes black & white.

Cast:
Michael Ansara as Deputy U.S. Marshal Sam Buckhart.
The theme song for this program was composed by Herschel Burke Gilbert.

Synopsis:
Lebanese-American Michael Ansara went from playing Apache chief Cochise on *Broken Arrow* to Deputy United States Marshal Sam Buckhart in *Law of The Plainsman*.

Buckhart had been born an Apache named Buck Heart. Following a raid, he rescued an Army captain and nursed him back to health.

When the captain died several years later, Buck Heart received his inheritance. Buck Heart went East to private schools, and eventually graduated from Harvard.

He then returned to his native West as Sam Buckhart, and became a Deputy U.S. Marshal. He served under Marshal Andy Morrison, and was based in Santa Fe, New Mexico.

Like *Broken Arrow* before it, *Law of the Plainsman* aimed for a more moderate view of the White Man – Native American struggles of the late 1800's.

The show had two pilots, both of which aired on *The Rifleman:* "The Indian," and "The Raid."

Lawman

1958 – 1962, ABC, 156 episodes all thirty minutes black & white.
Best Rating: 15th in 1960.

Cast:
John Russell as Marshal Dan Troop
Peter Brown as Deputy Johnny McKay
Peggy Castle as Lily Merrill (1959-1962)

The theme song for this program was composed by Jerry Livingston, with lyrics by David Mack. The performers are not credited.

Synopsis:
The "Lawman" was Dan Troop, marshal of Laramie, Wyoming, in the 1870s. Troop, portrayed by John Russell, was a no-nonsense peace officer, unyielding and commanding.

Playing off Troop's sternness was Peter Brown as Deputy Johnny McKay, younger and more of a free wheeler.

Troop became marshal when the former lawman was murdered. Troop hired McKay, and together they made the streets of Laramie safe through four years of straightforward, straight shooting episodes.

Peggy Castle's Lily Merrill, owner of the Birdcage Saloon, tried to help the tightly coiled marshal unwind.

Russell died in 1991, at age 70, Brown in 2016 at age 80. Castle died at age 45, in 1973.

MacKenzie's Raiders

Years: 1958 – 1959, Syndicated, 39 episodes all thirty minutes black & white.

Cast:

Richard Carlson as Colonel Ranald S. MacKenzie

The theme song for this program was composed by David Rose.

Synopsis:

The real Colonel Ranald S. MacKenzie was a calvary officer stationed on the Texas/Mexico border. In this series, MacKenzie and his Raiders chased Mexican bandits back and forth across that border. Art Gilmore provided narration.

Carlson died in 1977, at the age of 65.

Man from Blackhawk

1959 – 1960, ABC, 37 episodes all thirty minutes black & white.

Cast:

Robert Rockwell as Sam Logan

This series was created by Herb Meadow.

Synopsis:

As an insurance agent in the Old West, Sam Logan looked into fraud cases for the Blackhawk Insurance Company.

Rockwell died in 2003, at age 82.

Man Without a Gun

1957 – 1959, Syndicated, 52 episodes all thirty minutes black & white.

Cast:

Rex Reason as Adam MacLean
Mort Mills as Marshal Frank Tallman

The theme song is a version of "Red River Valley."

Synopsis:

Adam MacLean was a crusading newspaper editor who tried to clean up the Dakota Territory with words instead of a gun. Marshal Tallman was always nearby.

Reason died at age 86 in 2015, Mills age 74 in 1993.

Overland Trail

1960, NBC, 17 episodes all one-hour black & white.

Cast:

William Bendix as Frederick Thomas
Doug McClure as Flip Flippen

The theme song for this program was composed by Jeff Alexander, David Kahn, Stanley Wilson.

Synopsis:

This series told of the push to extend the Overland Trail from Missouri to California. Crusty Civil War veteran Frederick Thomas was in charge, assisted by his feisty young friend, Flip Flippen. Doug McClure, as Flip, gained training for *The Virginian* on this brief series.

Bendix died in 1964, at age 58.

Pony Express

1959 – 1960, Syndicated, 39 episodes all thirty minutes black & white.

Cast:
Grant Sullivan as Brett Clark
Don Dorell as Donovan

Synopsis:
Brett Clark was a troubleshooter for the Pony Express, and Donovan was a rider. Sullivan died at age 86, in 2011. Dorell died at age 49, in 1978.

Range Rider

1951 – 1953, Syndicated, 76 episodes all thirty minutes black & white.

Cast:
Jock Mahoney as the Range Rider
Dick Jones as Dick West
The theme song was the classic, "Home on the Range."

Synopsis:
Range Rider was similar to *The Lone Ranger* in that the "Rider's" identity was secret, the bad guys always lost, and the stories were action packed. Played by noted stuntman Jock Mahoney, the "Rider" didn't wear a mask.
Mahoney died in 1989 at age 79.

Rango

1967, ABC, 17 episodes all thirty minutes color.

Cast:
Tim Conway as Rango
Guy Marks as Pink Cloud

This program was created by Harvey Bullock and R.S. Allen. The theme song was composed by Earle Hagen and Ben Raleigh, and was performed by Frankie Laine.

Synopsis:

Tim Conway played inept Texas Ranger Rango in this brief series. Guy Marks was Native American Pink Cloud.

Rango, whose father was a commander of the Rangers, was assigned to the quiet Deep Wells Station to keep him from harm's way. Trouble, of course, seemed to follow.

Conway gained more fame for his comedic abilities on *The Carol Burnett Show*.

Conway died in 2019 at age 85, Marks died in 1987, at the age of 64.

Sara

1976, CBS, 12 episodes all one-hour color.

Cast:

Brenda Vaccaro as Sara Yarnell
Bert Kramer as Emmett Ferguson

This show was created by Michael Gleason. The theme song was composed by Lee Holdridge.

Synopsis:

In this atypical Western, young and single Sara leaves her boring Philadelphia life to become the teacher of a one-room school in Independence, Colorado.

Her students, and a few adults, appreciate Sara's efforts at education. Others, such as school board member Emmett Ferguson, don't appreciate her strong-willed ways.

A CBS television movie, *Territorial Men*, consisting of footage from the series, also aired in 1976.

Bert Kramer died at age 66, in 2001.

Saturday Roundup

1951, NBC, 12 episodes all one-hour black & white.

Cast:

Kermit Maynard.

Synopsis:

This anthology series told the stories of author James Oliver Curwood. Kermit Maynard, younger brother of cowboy movie star Ken Maynard, had the lead role in each episode.

The younger Maynard was a onetime world champion rodeo rider, and had also appeared in several 1930's Western motion pictures.

Maynard died at age 73, in 1971.

Shane

1966, ABC, 17 episodes all one-hour black & white.

Cast:

David Carradine as Shane
Jill Ireland as Marian Starett
This show was based upon the book and motion picture of the same name. The theme song was composed by Victor Young.

Synopsis:

After the character of Shane rode away at the end of the 1953 Western movie classic *Shane*, he returned thirteen years later in this television series.

The series enabled David Carradine to gain Western experience for his future role in *Kung Fu*.

Shotgun Slade

1959 – 1961, Syndicated, 78 episodes all thirty minutes black & white.

Cast:

    Scott Brady as Shotgun Slade

    This show was created by Frank Guber and the theme song composed by Gerald Fried.

Synopsis:

In this curious series, "Shotgun Slade" was a private detective in the Old West. Monica was his love interest. Jazzy background music was provided by Gerald Fried, and guest stars included individuals such as Sandy Koufax and Johnny Cash.

    Slade's distinctive weapon had a lower barrel which fired a 12-gauge shotgun shell, while its upper barrel fired a .32-caliber rifle bullet.

    The show's pilot aired on CBS's *Schlitz Playhouse*.

    Scott Brady died in 1985, at age 60.

Stagecoach West

1960 – 1961, ABC, 38 episodes all sixty minutes black & white.

Cast:

    Wayne Rogers as Luke Perry
    Robert Bray as Simon Kane

    The theme song for this program was composed by Skip Martin with lyrics by Terry Gilkyson. The song was performed by the folk music duo Bud and Travis.

Synopsis:

Luke Perry, played by Wayne Rogers a decade before he became Trapper John in *M*A*S*H*, and Simon Kane were stage drivers.

    The characters they met, the outlaws and Native Americans they fought, difficulties with the stage, horses, and weather, and superb guest stars, carried the tales.

    Rogers died in 2015 at age 82, Kane in 1983 at age 65.

Steve Donovan, Western Marshal

1955 – 1956, Syndicated, 39 episodes all thirty minutes black & white.

Cast:
Douglas Kennedy as Marshal Steve Donovan
Eddy Waller as Deputy Rusty Lee

This series was filmed in 1951 as *Steve Donovan, Western Ranger*. After performing poorly in a limited market, the show was given a new title and released again four years later, to better success.

Synopsis:
This action-packed show was set in 1870s Wyoming, where Marshal Donovan and Deputy Lee tried to keep the territory safe for honest citizens.
Western veteran Douglas Kennedy was excellent in the lead role.
Kennedy died at age 57, in 1973, Waller died at age 88, in 1977.

Stories of the Century

1954 – 1955, Syndicated, 39 episodes all thirty minutes black & white.

Cast:
Jim Davis as Matt Clark
Mary Castle as Frankie Adams
Kristine Miller as Jonesy Jones

The theme song for this program was composed by Herschel Burke Gilbert.

Synopsis:
Stories of the Century followed the adventures onboard a trans-continental railroad, of which Matt Clark is a detective. His partner – unique considering when this show was made – was a woman. Frankie Adams was first, then Jonesy Jones.

In a prominent theme, Clark and his partner had to deal with virtually every well-known outlaw in the real West.

Davis, who also narrated, died at age 71, in 1981. Castle died at age 67, in 1998, Miller age 90, in 2015.

Sugarfoot

1957 – 1961, ABC, 69 episodes all one-hour black & white.

Cast:

Will Hutchins as Tom "Sugarfoot" Brewster

Best ratings: 21st in 1959, 23rd in 1958.
This series was created by Michael Fessier.
The pilot was a remake of the *The Boy from Oklahoma*, a Western film released in 1954 which starred Will Rogers Jr., as Brewster.
The theme song was composed by Mack David and Jay Livingston. The performers are not credited.

Synopsis:

Sugarfoot, along with *Bronco*, was developed to fill the void when *Cheyenne's* Clint Walker and Warner Brothers Studios had difficulties.
It alternated with the other two series.
Sugarfoot was a name given to someone greener than a tenderfoot, such as law student Tom Brewster.
Brewster rode the West studying law by correspondence, doing odd jobs, nabbing outlaws, and dancing with a few ladies, all with a smile on his face and with a sense of humor.
Hutchins returned to character in 1993, hosting the *TV's Western Heroes* video.

Tales of the Texas Rangers

1955 – 1958, ABC and CBS, 52 episodes all thirty minutes black & white.

Cast:

Willard Parker as Ranger Jace Pearson
Harry Lauter as Ranger Clay Morgan

This series was based upon a radio program of the same name. The theme song, "These are Tales of the Texas Rangers," was sung to the tune of "The Eyes of Texas are Upon You."

Synopsis:

The time frame of this series ranged from the 1830s, when the Rangers began, to the 1950s, when this show was produced. Rangers Jace Pearson and Clay Morgan appeared each week as themselves, or their grandfathers, in different adventures and different settings.

The radio program had Texas Ranger Captain Manual Gonzaullas as an actual consultant. Although given similar credit on the television show, the stories were not as factual as what had been on radio.

Parker died at age 84 in 1996, Lauter age 76 in 1990.

Temple Houston

1963 – 1964, NBC, 26 episodes all one-hour black & white.

Cast:

Jeffrey Hunter as Temple Houston
Jack Elam as Marshal George Taggard

The theme song was "The Yellow Rose of Texas," as arranged by Frank Comstock and Ned Washington.

Synopsis:

This show was based upon real-life frontier lawyer, Temple Houston. The son of Sam Houston, Temple Houston had two children living when the show aired.

The pilot episode was not shown on television. Rather it was released as the feature film *Man from Galveston* (even though it was less than an hour long), with James Coburn as Marshal Taggard.

Temple Houston was rushed into production in four weeks, which was an unheard-of feat. The show ranged from being a Western legal drama to a comedy.

Hunter died at age 42, in 1969.

Tate

1960, NBC, 13 episodes all thirty minutes black & white.

Cast:
David McLean as Tate
This series was created by Harry Julian Fink.

Synopsis:
The man known as Tate had his left arm crippled in the Civil War, and was forced to carry it sheathed in leather.

But Tate's right arm worked fine, as he used his fast draw numerous times roaming the West as a bounty hunter in this grim series. With his useless arm, Tate was the first disabled lead character on television.

McLean, well-known as the "Marlboro Man," died in 1995 at the age of 73.

Texas John Slaughter

1958 – 1961 ABC, 15 episodes all one-hour black & white. This program was originally called "Tales of Texas John Slaughter."

Cast:
Tom Tryon as John Slaughter
The theme song for this program was composed by Stan Jones.
Narration by Paul Frees.

Synopsis:
Texas John Slaughter aired its fifteen episodes over three seasons of *Walt Disney Presents*.

The show was based upon the real-life John Slaughter, a Civil War veteran turned Texas Ranger turned sheriff in 1880s Texas. The character wore a large white cowboy hat with the front brim pinned up.

Tryon became a successful novelist using the name Thomas Tryon. He died in 1991 at the age of 65.

The Adventures of Champion

1955 – 1956, CBS 26 episodes all thirty minutes black and white.

Cast:
Barry Curtis as Ricky North

This program was based upon a radio show of the same name. The theme song was composed by Norman Luboff, with lyrics by Marilyn Bergman and performed by Frankie Laine.

Synopsis:

This children's program featured 12-year-old Ricky having adventures with Champion the stallion, with assistance from Rebel the German shepherd.

Champion was the leader of a wild horse herd, with Ricky being the only person the horse would let ride. The horse belonged to Gene Autry, and the two appeared together in several films.

The Adventures of Judge Roy Bean

1955 – 1956, Syndicated, 39 episodes all thirty minutes in color.

Cast:

Edgar Buchanan as Judge Roy Bean

The theme song, "Law of the Pecos," was written by Eddie Paul, Roy Ingraham, and Charles Koff.

Synopsis:

Edgar Buchanan, later to be Uncle Joe on *Petticoat Junction*, was a hoot as real-life Judge Roy Bean, who had proclaimed himself the "Law West of the Pecos."

Buchanan died in 1979 at the age of 76.

The Adventures of Kit Carson

1951 – 1955, Syndicated, 104 episodes all thirty minutes black & white.

Cast:

Bill Williams as Kit Carson
Don Diamond as El Toro

Synopsis:

This children's program featured legendary scout Kit Carson and sidekick Don Diamond helping those in need. Diamond was later to become Crazy Cat on *F Troop*.

Each episode was introduced by Hank Paterson, talking to a group of children drinking Coke, the show's sponsor.

Williams died at age 77 in 1992, Diamond aged 90 in 2011.

The Alaskans

1959 – 1960, ABC, 37 episodes all one-hour black & white.

Cast:

Roger Moore as Silky Harris
Jeff York as Reno McKee

The theme song for this program was composed by Mack David and Jerry Livingston.

Synopsis:

Set in Skagway, Alaska, this program had Harris and McKee attempting to swindle those bound for the Yukon Territories during the Klondike Gold Rush.

Moore died in 2017 at age 89, York in 1995 at age 83.

The Big Valley

1965 – 1969, ABC, 112 episodes all one-hour color.

Cast:

Barbara Stanwyck as Victoria Barkley
Linda Evans as Audra Barkley
Richard Long as Jarrod Barkley
Peter Breck as Nick Barkley
Lee Majors as Heath Barkley

Charles Briles appeared in season one as the youngest son, Eugene. The character was written out of the series when Briles was drafted into the military.

This series was created by A.I. Bezzerides and Louis Edelman, the theme song composed by George Duning.

Synopsis:

The Barkley Ranch in the San Joaquin Valley of 1870's California was the setting for this four-year Western.

Long time movie star Barbara Stanwyck was matriarch Victoria Barkley, a single parent seeing over a ranch and house full of grown, unmarried children.

Although this scenario was familiar to viewers, the program's creators insisted the series was based upon the massive Hill Ranch of that area.

Young, beautiful Linda Evans was daughter Audra. Peter Breck (*The Black Saddle*) played son and quick-tempered ranch foreman Nick. Richard Long (*77 Sunset Strip*) was the eldest son and attorney Jarrod.

Lee Majors, in his first series, played Heath, the illegitimate son of Victoria's late husband, Tom, and a Native American woman. The Barkleys took him in and gave him their name. The cook for this crew was Napoleon Whiting as Silas.

As with other frontier families, the Barkleys fought land grabbers, other ranchers, bank robbers, murderers, con men, Native Americans, and Mexicans.

With an excellent cast and strong production values, *The Big Valley* was a notch above many contemporaries. The program is also noted as being the only adult Western built around a female lead. Despite all this, the show never broke television's top twenty-five.

Evans appeared (not as Audra) in a pair of Kenny Rogers *Gambler* productions, *The Adventure Continues* and *Luck of the Draw*.

Stanwyck died at age 82, in 1990; Long at age 47 in 1974; Breck at age 82 in 2012; Briles at age 70, in 2016.

The Black Saddle

1959 – 1960, NBC 20 episodes, ABC 24 episodes, all thirty minutes black & white.

Cast:
Peter Breck as Clay Culhane
Russell Johnson as Marshal Gib Scott

This series was created by Hal Hudson and John McGreevy. The theme song was composed by Herschel Burke Gilbert and Arthur Morton.

Synopsis:

Peter Breck, several years away from becoming a Barkley brother in *The Big Valley*, played Clay Culhane. He came from a family of gunfighters, and was a gunslinger himself.

After his two brothers were killed in a shootout, Clay changed occupations. He studied law, and upon graduation returned to the New Mexico territory. Clay traveled about, law books in the saddlebags of his black saddle, providing assistance to those in need.

Johnson, later to become lost on *Gilligan's Island*, was Marshal Gib Scott. Johnson died in 2014 at age 89.

The Californians

1957 – 1959, NBC, 69 episodes, all thirty minutes black & white.

Cast:

Adam Kennedy as Dion Patrick
Sean McClory as Jack McGivern

This series was created by Louis Edelman and Robert F. Sisk. The theme song was composed by Harry Warren and Harold Adamson.

Synopsis:

San Francisco during and after the gold rush of 1849 was rough and rowdy, causing crusading newspaperman Dion Patrick and general store owner Jack McGivern to form and lead a group of vigilantes.

Richard Coogan as lawman Matthew Wayne soon arrived.

Sponsorship interference led to cast turnover and a change from the vigilante theme to more typical stories, and eventually cancellation.

Coogan died in 2014 at age 99, Kennedy in 1997 at age 75, McClory in 2003 at age 79.

The Chisholms

1980 CBS, 13 episodes, one hour long in color.

Cast:
Robert Preston as Hadley Chisholm
Rosemary Harris as Minerva Chisholm
Ben Murphy as Will Chisholm

This show was created by David Dortort and developed by Evan Hunter.

Synopsis:
The Chisholms first appeared as a mini-series in 1979, with the clan moving from Virginia to California. In the short-lived 1980 series the family was still heading West, this time with a wagon train.

The large cast was led by Preston and Harris as the parents, and Murphy as oldest son Will. Preston's character died midway through the show's run, and the actor passed away in 1987 at age 68.

Murphy previously co-starred in *Alias Smith & Jones*.

The Dakotas

1963, ABC, 19 episodes all one-hour black & white.

Cast:
Larry Ward as Marshal Frank Ragan
Jack Elam as Deputy J.D. Smith
Chad Everett as Deputy Del Stark
Mike Greene as Deputy Vance Porter

The theme song for this program was composed by William Lava.

Synopsis:
The Dakotas started its run in January, 1963, after *Cheyenne* had concluded the previous month. The pilot episode had aired more than a year earlier, in that time slot.

This particularly adult series was set in the Dakota Territory after the Civil War. The Black Hills and Badlands were overrun with violent men, and the "Dakota" lawmen met them head on in tense, action filled, violent episodes.

Larry Ward was the terse Marshal Ragan. He wore an eye patch in the pilot, explaining that after a gunfight, "I woke up blind in one eye." In the series, the patch was gone.

Deputies were Jack Elam, perfectly cast as a former gunfighter; Chad Everett in his first starring role, and lanky Michael Greene.

The Dakotas was abruptly cancelled after 19 episodes. The 18th episode, "Sanctuary at Crystal Springs," featured a violent gun battle inside a church which resulted in severe criticism from viewers. ABC yielded, and after one more episode, *The Dakotas* ended. A twentieth episode, "Black Gold," never aired.

This superb show, with realistic characterizations, intricate stories, and a raw depiction of the period's brutality, overwhelmed its audience.

Ward died in 1985 at age 60, Elam in 2003 at age 82, Everett in 2012 at age 75.

The Deputy

1959 – 1961, NBC, 76 episodes all thirty minutes black & white.

Cast:

Henry Fonda as Marshal Simon Fry
Allen Case as Deputy Clay McCord

This series was created by Roland Kibbee and Norman Lear. The theme song was composed by Jack Marshal.

Synopsis:

Movie star Henry Fonda served as narrator for this show.

He appeared sparsely in most episodes, occasionally taking the lead role. As the title indicated, the focus on *The Deputy* was just that: part time deputy Clay McCord. A storekeeper, McCord became a full-time deputy in season two.

Fonda died in 1982 at age 77, Case in 1986 at age 51.

The Gabby Hayes Show

1950 – 1954, NBC, fifteen-minute episodes; 1958, ABC, thirty-minute episodes. All episodes were black and white.

Cast:
George "Gabby" Hayes

Synopsis:
Popular Western sidekick Gabby Hayes hosted this children's production in which he talked to an audience of kids, narrated clips from Western movies, or both.

Fred Rogers – later to become immortalized in *Mister Rogers's Neighborhood* – was the floor manager of this program until 1953, when he left to work in public television.

The Gabby Hayes Show received an Emmy nomination in 1953 for Children's Programming. Sponsored by Quaker Oates, Hayes would fire a small cannon loaded with puffed cereal at the camera.

Hayes died in 1969, at age 83.

The Guns of Will Sonnett

1967 – 1969, ABC, 50 episodes, all thirty minutes color.

Cast:
Walter Brennan as Will Sonnett
Dack Rambo as Jeff Sonnett
Jason Evers as Jim Sonnett

This series was created by Aaron Spelling and Richard Carr. The theme song was composed by Hugo Friedhofer.

Synopsis:
The distinctive premise of this show had retired Army scout Will Sonnet and his grown grandson, Jeff, searching the West for Jeff's father, James.

James had left his family twenty years earlier and was a gunfighter, on the run. They found James in the last episode. James renounced his gunfighting ways, and the family trio became lawmen.

The highly acclaimed Brennan is considered to be one of the finest character actors in television and movie history. A veteran of World War 1, he appeared in more than 230 movie and television roles during a career spanning five decades, and was the first actor to win three Academy Awards.

Brennan was also successful in the music industry, with "Old Rivers" reaching number five on Billboard.

Brennan died in 1974, at the age of 80. Evers died in 2005 at age 83.

The High Chaparral

1967 – 1971 NBC, 98 episodes all one-hour color.

Cast:
Leif Erickson as John Cannon
Cameron Mitchell as Buck Cannon
Mark Slade as Billy Blue Cannon (1967-1970)
Henry Darrow as Manolito Montoya
Linda Cristal as Victoria Cannon
Frank Silvera as Don Sebastian Montoya (1967-1970)

This series was created by David Dortort and theme song composed by David Rose.

Synopsis:
After eight years of producing *Bonanza*, producer David Dortort became the Cartwright's executive producer as he created and produced this Western for NBC.

The High Chaparral was the name of the ranch owned by Big John Cannon, played by Leif Erickson, on the Mexican border in 1870s Arizona Territory.

The show told the story of his determination to make the ranch into a cattle empire, no matter what Apaches, outlaws, other ranchers, and even the Army, could do to impede.

When Cannon's wife was killed by Apaches, he formed an alliance with Don Sebastian Montoya, whose ranch met John's at the border. Cannon married Montoya's daughter, Victoria, who was thirty years younger. The two land owners then combined their efforts to keep the Apaches at bay.

Others on the ranch were Cannon's son, Billy Blue, his brother, Buck, and Manolito Montoya, who followed his sister across the border.

The High Chaparral provided solid Western entertainment, but during its four seasons never broke into the top twenty-five.

Erickson died in 1986 at age 74, Mitchell in 1994 at age 75, Silvera in 1970 at age 55.

The Legend of Jesse James

1965 – 1966, ABC, 34 episodes all thirty minutes black & white.

Cast:

Christopher Jones as Jesse James
Allen Case as Frank James
John Milford as Cole Younger
Robert Wilkes as Marshal Sam Corbett

This series was created by Samuel Peeples. The theme song was composed by Ken Darby, with lyrics by Irvin Gertz and performed by a studio choir.

Synopsis:

At 2 o'clock on a February afternoon in 1866, Jessie James led the James and Younger outlaw gang into Liberty, Missouri. There, they committed the nation's first bank robbery, murdering George Wymore in the process.

This was the first of more than two dozen bank, train, and stagecoach robberies which the gang committed.

This highly fictionalized show portrayed them as Robin Hoods.

Jones died in 2014 at age 72, Milford in 2000 at age 70, Wilkes in 1979 at age 74.

The Loner

1965 – 1966, CBS, 26 episodes all thirty minutes black & white.

Cast:

Lloyd Bridges as William Colton

This series was created by Rod Serling and the theme song composed by Jerry Goldsmith.

Synopsis:
The highly respected series featured Lloyd Bridges as Civil War veteran William Colton. Sick of the killing, he headed West.

Somber, focusing on characterization with themes of morals, religion, and bigotry, *The Loner* was an unconventional Western.

Serling, fresh off his award-winning *Twilight Zone* series, wrote many of the scripts.

Bridges, four years removed from *Sea Hunt*, agreed to return to weekly television because of the excellent program he knew Serling and noted TV executive William Dozier would produce.

In spite of the show's qualities, *The Loner* did not attract a large enough audience to be renewed for a second season.

Bridges died at age 85, in 1998.

The Marshal of Gunsight Pass

1950, ABC, 29 episodes all thirty minutes black & white.

Cast:
Russell Hayden
Eddie Dean

This show was based upon a radio program of the same name.

Synopsis:
In this obscure children's show, Hayden and Dean were marshals. The program was broadcast live, from an indoor set. Hayden died in 1981 at age 68, Dean in 1991 at age 91.

The Monroes

1966 – 1967, ABC, 26 episodes all one-hour color.

Cast:
Michael Anderson, Jr. as Clayt Monroe
Barbara Hershey as Kathy Monroe

Keith Schultz as Jefferson Monroe
Kevin Schultz as Fennimore Monroe
Tammy Locke as Amy Monroe

This series was created by Milt Rosen.

Synopsis:

The Monroe family were on their way to Wyoming to lay claim to land the father, Albert, had staked out earlier. But an accident in the Snake River claimed the lives of Albert and his wife, Mary.

That left their five children, led by 18-year-old Clayt and 16-year-old Kathy, to either carry on or turn back. The Monroe children pressed on and started working the land, dealing with numerous difficulties along the way.

The show was filmed on location, near the Grand Teton National Park.

The Nine Lives of Elfego Baca

1958 – 1960, ABC, ten episodes, all one-hour black & white.

Cast:

Robert Loggia as Elfego Baca
This semi-continuing series was presented on *Walt Disney Presents*.

Synopsis:

This show was based upon the real-life Elfego Baca, who was said to have nine lives after surviving as a lawman in New Mexico. He eventually became a lawyer. Some of the stories were based upon actual events.

Loggia died in 2015 at age 85.

The Outcasts

1968 – 1969, ABC, 26 episodes, all one-hour color.

Cast:

Don Murray as Earl Corey
Otis Young as Jemal David

The Outcasts was created by Ben Brady and Leon Tokatyan. The theme was composed by Hugo Montenegro.

Synopsis:
In a series ahead of its time, ex-slave owner Earl Corey finds himself teamed with ex-slave Jemal David in the Old West after the Civil War. The two formed an uneasy partnership as bounty hunters in this well-written, tense program.

Young died in 2001, at age 69.

The Outlaws

1960 – 1962, NBC, 50 episodes all one-hour black and white.

Cast:
Barton MacLane as Marshal Frank Caine
Don Collier as Deputy, and Marshal, Will Foreman
Jock Gaynor as Heck Martin
Bruce Yarnall as Deputy Chalk Breeson
Slim Pickens as Slim
Judy Lewis as Connie Masters

Synopsis:
Although *The Outlaws* was on two seasons, it was like two different shows. During the first year, stories were told from the outlaws' point of view. Year two, with an almost new cast, shifted to traditional storytelling.

MacLane died in 1969, at age 66, Gaynor in 1998 at age 69, Yarnell in 1973 at age 35, Lewis in 2011 at age 76.

The Quest

1976 NBC, 15 episodes (although only 11 aired) one hour in color.

Cast:
Kurt Russell as Morgan "Two Persons" Beaudine
Tim Matheson as Quentin Beaudine

This show was created by Tracy Keenan Wynn.

Synopsis:

The Beaudine brothers, played by Russell and Matheson, searched the West for their sister Patricia. Matheson's character was educated, whereas Russell's Morgan and their sister had been taken by the Cheyenne years earlier. Morgan even had a Cheyenne name.

Matheson was three years removed from his brief stint on *Bonanza*, and Russell went on to movie stardom.

The Rebel

1959 – 1961, ABC, 76 episodes all thirty minutes black & white.

Cast:

Nick Adams as Johnny Yuma

This series was created by Andrew J. Fenady and Nick Adams. The theme song was composed by Richard Markowitz, with lyrics by Andrew J. Fenady. Johnny Cash performed the song.

Synopsis:

The Rebel is the saga of Johnny Yuma, an ex-Confederate who roamed the West after the Civil War. In addition to his pistol, Yuma carried his deceased father's sawed-off shotgun. He also wanted to become a writer, so he kept a journal of his adventures.

Nick Adams, somewhat of a youth idol at the time, had his friend Elvis Presley record the title song. The producers, however, favored the Cash version.

Adams died at the age of 36, in 1968.

The Restless Gun

1957 – 1959, NBC, 77 episodes all thirty minutes black & white.

Cast:

John Payne as Vint Bonner
Best Rating: 8th in 1958.

This series is derived from the Jimmy Stewart 1953 radio program, *The Six Shooter*, which was created by Frank Burt. In the radio show the lead character was named Britt Ponset.

Synopsis:
Vint Bonner and his restless gun roamed from town to town, looking for a place to settle. This show was very popular during its first season, and NBC wanted to expand it to one hour. Payne declined, the ratings fell during the second year, and the show was cancelled.

The pilot had aired on the *CBS Schlitz Playhouse of the Stars*.

When *The Restless Gun* ended, producer David Dortort created a more popular Western, *Bonanza*.

Payne died in 1989, at age 79.

The Road West

1966 – 1967, NBC, 26 episodes all one-hour color.

Cast:
Barry Sullivan as Benjamin Pride
Kelly Corcoran as Kip Pride
Andrew Prine as Timothy Pride
Brenda Scott as Midge Pride

Synopsis:
Following the Civil War, widower Benjamin Pride uprooted his family and headed to Kansas. Numerous hardships, of course, were encountered.

Sullivan died in 1994 at age 81, Corcoran in 2002 at age 43.

The Rough Riders

1958 – 1959, ABC, 39 episodes all thirty minutes black & white.

Cast:
Kent Taylor as Jim Flagg
Jan Merlin as Colin Kirby
Peter Whitney as Buck Sinclair
The theme song was composed by Cliff Radford.

Synopsis:

After the Civil War, ex-Confederate soldier Colin Kirby teamed with ex-Union soldiers Jim Flagg and Buck Sinclair to head West to have more adventures and seek their fortune.

Taylor died at age 79 in 1987, Merlin age 94 in 2019, Whitney age 55 in 1972.

The Rounders

1966 – 1967, ABC, 17 episodes all thirty minutes color.

Cast:

Ron Hayes as Ben Jones
Chill Wills as Jim Ed Love
Patrick Wayne as Howdy Lewis

The show was based upon a 1966 movie of the same name. The theme song was composed by Jeff Alexander.

Synopsis:

This Western comedy co-starred John Wayne's son, Patrick, as Howdy who worked alongside Hayes' Ben for shady ranch owner Love, played by Wills.

Hayes died at age 75 in 2004, Wills age 75 in 1978.

The Tall Man

1960 – 1962, NBC, 75 episodes all thirty minutes black & white.

Cast:

Clu Gulager as William "Billy the Kid" Bonney
Barry Sullivan as Sheriff Pat Garrett

This series was created by Samuel Peeples. The theme song was composed by Juan Esquivel.

Synopsis:

The Tall Man was 6'3" Barry Sullivan as Pat Garrett, sheriff of volatile Lincoln County, New Mexico.

In this remake of Western history, Garrett and the infamous Billy the Kid (Gulager) became friends. In real life, Garrett ambushed and shot the Kid.

Although highly fictionalized, *The Tall Man* featured plenty of action but lacked a conclusion to the Garrett – Kid story.

Sullivan died at the age of 81, in 1994.

The Texan

1958 – 1960, CBS, 78 episodes all thirty minutes black & white.

Cast:

Rory Calhoun as Bill Longley
Best Rating: 15th in 1959.

Synopsis:

In the real West, Bill Longley became a killer at age 15 and was hanged at age 27.

Star and co-producer Rory Calhoun cleaned up the character for this series but was still able to find adventure, and even occasional romance, as he wandered Texas.

In a rarity for its time, season two had several multi-part stories.

Calhoun died at the age of 76, in 1999.

The Travels of Jaimie McPheeters

1963 – 1964, ABC, 26 episodes all one-hour black & white.

Cast:

Kurt Russell as Jaimie McPheeters
Dan O'Herlihy as Doc McPheeters
Charles Bronson as Linc Murdock

The Osmond Brothers as the singing Kissel brothers, Micah, Deuteronomy, Lamentations, and Leviticus

This series was based upon the Pulitzer Prize-winning novel by Robert Lewis Taylor. The show's theme song was composed by Leigh Harline and Jerry Winn, and was performed by the Osmond Brothers.

Synopsis:

A wagon train heading to California was the stage for future movie star Kurt Russell as young Jaimie McPheeters, traveling with his father "Doc," played by Dan O'Herlihy.

Charles Bronson – also soon to be a movie star – joined the cast midway through the season as wagon master Linc Murdock.

As to be expected, the wagon train was composed of and met a wide array of colorful characters. The last episode, "The Day of Reckoning," was expanded into the 1964 movie *Guns of Diablo*, with Russell and Bronson reprising their roles.

O'Herlihy died in 2005 at age 85, Bronson in 2003 at age 81.

The Westerner

1960, NBC, 13 episodes all thirty minutes black & white.

Cast:

Brian Keith as Dave Blassingame

This series was created by Sam Peckinpah. The theme song was composed by Herschel Burke Gilbert.

Synopsis:

The Westerner is one of the most underrated series in the television West. Dave Blassingame, realistically portrayed by Brian Keith, roamed the West with his dog, Brown, looking for jobs and having adventures.

With Peckinpah directing and co-writing several episodes, the show was uncompromising. Perhaps the audience at the time was not ready for such adult fare, as the program was cancelled midway through the first season.

Comic relief was provided for three episodes by John Dehner, as dapper Burgundy Smith.

The pilot, "Trouble at Tres Cruces," aired on *Dick Powell's Zane Grey Theater*. In 1963, *Zane Grey* aired an updated, revived version of the show, *The Losers*, with Lee Marvin, which failed to attract network interest.

The episode, "Line Camp," was the basis for the 1968 motion picture, *Will Penny*. Keith reprised the character of Dave Blassingame in the 1991 mini-series, *Luck of the Draw*, starring Kenny Rogers.

Keith died at age 75, in 1997.

The Wild Wild West

1965 – 1969, CBS, 104 episodes one hour; twenty-eight in black & white, seventy-six in color.

Cast:
Robert Conrad as James T. West
Ross Martin as Artemus Gordon
Best Rating: 23rd in 1966.

This series was created by Michael Garrison. The theme song was composed by Richard Markowitz.

Synopsis:
Robert Conrad as James T. West and Ross Martin as Artemus Gordon were undercover agents for President Ulysses S. Grant. Their assignments consisted of protecting Grant, solving crimes, and exposing various groups who were trying to take over the United States, or even the world.

The Wild, Wild West featured a mixture of humor, adventure, special effects, interesting props, and an outstanding collection of villains, the best being Dr. Miguelito Loveless, played by Michael Dunn. Martin, as Gordon, was a master of disguises.

The program had two reunion movies, *The Wild Wild West Revisited* in 1979, and *More Wild Wild West*, in 1980.

A motion picture starring Will Smith and Kevin Kline was released in 1999; other than the title and names of characters, the movie had little in common with the television program.

Conrad died at age 84 in 2020, Martin at age 61 in 1981.

Tombstone Territory

1957 – 1959 ABC, 1959 – 1960 Syndicated, 91 episodes all thirty minutes black & white.

Cast:

Pat Conway as Sheriff Clay Hollister
Richard Eastham as Harris Calibourne

The theme song, "Whistle Me Up a Memory," was written and performed by William Backer.

Synopsis:

Stories for this show were taken from newspaper articles which had been published in the Tombstone Epitaph newspaper.

Although Sheriff Hollister and the newspaper editor, Calibourne, were fictional, numerous historical characters were used.

After a two-year run on ABC, production continued another season for syndication.

Conway died in 1981 at the age of 50. Eastham, who provided narration, died in 2005 at age 89.

Trackdown

1957 – 1959, CBS, 71 episodes all thirty minutes black & white.

Cast:

Robert Culp as Hoby Gilman

This series was created by John Robinson and the theme song composed by William Loose and John Seely.

Synopsis:

Robert Culp made his television debut in this series as a Texas Ranger. His character, Hoby Gilman, initially travelled to different towns, tracking fugitives. By the middle of season one, he had settled in Porter, Texas.

The pilot, "Badge of Honor," aired on *Dick Powell's Zane Grey Theater*. And the series, *Wanted Dead or Alive*, was derived from the *Trackdown* episode, "The Bounty Hunter."

Culp, later to co-star in *I Spy*, died at age 79, in 2010.

26 Men

1957 – 1959, Syndicated, 87 episodes all thirty minutes black & white.

Cast:

Tris Coffin as Captain Thomas Harbo Rynning, who narrated many episodes (Running was a real-life captain in the Arizona Rangers)

Kelo Henderson as Ranger Clint Travis

The theme song for this program was composed by Hal Hooper and Russell Hayden, who wrote the lyrics.

Synopsis:

Filmed on location, this exceptionally popular syndicated program took its stories from the files of the Arizona Rangers, whose size was limited to twenty-six men.

Four retired rangers who had served under Captain Rynning introduced various episodes. Rynning was portrayed by Tris Coffin.

Kelo Henderson, who played Travis, was unparalleled in his expertise with a pistol. A foreman on a California ranch, Henderson was renowned throughout the area as an expert horseman, marksman, and quick-draw artist.

His notoriety with a pistol attracted the attention of Hollywood producers, and he was asked to audition for *26 Men*. Henderson displayed his abilities, and was immediately hired.

Upon being cast as Travis, the script for the first episode, "The Recruit," was changed to include two instances of gunplay for Henderson.

Following *26 Men*, Henderson performed sporadically until the mid 1960s, when he retired from acting in order to raise horses.

Henderson died in 2019 at age 96. Coffin died in 1990 at age 80.

Two Faces West

1960 – 1961, Syndicated, 39 episodes all thirty minutes black & white.

Cast:

Charles Bateman as Ben and Rick January

This program was inspired by the 1939 motion picture of the same name, and was created by Donald Gold and Jonas Seinfield.

Synopsis:

Charles Bateman played identical twins Rick and Ben January in the small town of Gunnison, Colorado. Rick was a quick-tempered gunfighter and Ben an easygoing doctor, who was as fast on the draw as his brother.

Union Pacific

1958, Syndicated, 39 episodes all thirty minutes black & white.

Cast:

Jeff Morrow as Bart McClelland
Judd Pratt as Bill Kinkaid
Susan Cummings as Georgia

This series was created by Robert Cinader and inspired by the 1939 motion picture of the same name.

Synopsis:

This program featured the troubles of the *Union Pacific,* the railroad which linked the country. McClelland was the supervisor, Kinkaid the surveyor, and Cummings the owner of the rolling Golden Nugget Saloon.

Morrow died in 1993 at age 86, Pratt in 2002 at age 85, Cummings in 2016 at age 86.

Wanted Dead or Alive

1958 – 1961, CBS, 94 episodes all thirty minutes black & white.

Cast:
Steve McQueen as Josh Randall

Best Ratings: 9th in 1960, 16th in 1959.
The theme song for the first season was composed by William Loose. The theme for the second and third seasons was composed by Herschel Burke Gilbert.

Synopsis:
Future movie icon Steve McQueen became a television star in this impressive series, playing bounty hunter Josh Randall. Literate scripts, limited Western clichés, and the charismatic McQueen combined for a three-year run of quality shows.

This program featured one of the television West's more distinctive guns, a Winchester Model 92 carbine which was sawed off at both ends, with an enlarged lever. McQueen called the gun a "Mare's Leg," and wore it as a belt gun. To increase the effect .44-.40 cartridges – too large for the gun – were worn in the cartridge belt.

Randall had a partner for eleven episodes, Wright King as Jason Nichols.

The 1987 motion picture, *Wanted: Dead or Alive*, resurrected the series, in a sense, as Rutger Hauer played modern bounty hunter Nick Randall, grandson of Josh.

McQueen died at age 50, in 1980.

Whiplash

1960 – 1961, Syndicated, 34 episodes all thirty minutes black & white.

Cast:
Peter Graves as Chris Cobb

This series was created by Michael Noonan and Michael Plant. The theme song was composed by Irwin Astley and performed by Frank Ifield.

Synopsis:

This show, produced in England, told of the development and dangers encountered by the 19th century Australian stage line Cobb & Company.

Peter Graves played American emigrant Chris Cobb, whose first name in real life was Freeman. He was proficient with a pistol, but preferred using a bullwhip.

Whiplash was enriched by location filming in Australia, including the use of kangaroos in the background. Writers included the noted Gene Rodenberry and Harry Julian Fink.

Graves died at age 80, in 2010.

Whispering Smith

1961, NBC, 26 episodes all thirty minutes black & white.

Cast:

Audie Murphy as Tom "Whispering" Smith

This program was inspired by a 1948 movie of the same name, which had been based upon a book of that name by Frank Spearman. The theme song was composed by Richard Shores.

Synopsis:

The stories in this series were taken from the files of the Denver Police Department. "Whispering Smith" was Detective Tom Smith of Denver, who used scientific methods, along with guns and fists, to catch criminals.

The show started filming in 1959, but didn't air until 1961.

Audie Murphy appeared in more than forty films during his career, several times receiving star billing. Most of his films were in the Western genre. *Whispering Smith* was his lone venture into television.

A veteran of World War II, Murphy received more than twenty medals for his actions, including the Medal of Honor.

Murphy died in 1971, at age 45.

Wichita Town

1959 – 1960, NBC, 26 episodes all thirty minutes black & white.

Cast:
Joel McCrea as Marshal Mike Dunbar
Jody McCrea as Deputy Ben Matheson

This series was derived from McCrea's 1955 film, *Wichita*.

Synopsis:
Long time Western film star Joel McCrea and his son, Jody, played marshal and deputy in this short-lived series set in Wichita, Kansas.
Joel McCrea died in 1990 at age 84, Jody McCrea in 2009 at age 74.

Wild Bill Hickok

1951 – 1958, Syndicated. 113 episodes all thirty minutes, both black & white and color.

Cast:
Guy Madison as James Butler "Wild Bill" Hickok
Andy Devine as Jingles B. Jones

Synopsis:
Wild Bill Hickok is an Old West legend who was murdered in Deadwood.
Although this "Kiddie Western" bore no resemblance to reality, the show was a success and in 1954 received an Emmy nomination for Best Western or Adventure Series. It lost to *Stories of the Century*.
Guy Madison, later to become *Zorro*, played Wild Bill. His rasping sidekick, Jingles, was played by Western movie veteran Andy Devine.
Madison died at age 74 in 1996, Devine at age 71 in 1977.

Wrangler

1960, NBC, 6 episodes all thirty minutes black & white.

Cast:

Jason Evers as Pitcairn the Wrangler

Synopsis:

In this series, Pitcairn the wrangler roamed the West having various escapades.

The show is noted for receiving an Emmy nomination for Outstanding Achievement in Electronic Camerawork.

Evers died in 2005, at age 83.

Yancy Derringer

1958 – 1959, CBS, 34 episodes all thirty minutes black & white.

Cast:

Jock Mahoney as Yancy Derringer
X. Brands as Pahoo-Ka-Ta-Wah

This series was based upon a short story by Richard Sale, and was created by Sale and Mary Loos.

Synopsis:

Yancy Derringer was a former Confederate officer living in New Orleans. He owned a riverboat, was a professional gambler, and was an undercover agent for the city. His gun of choice, of course, was a derringer. He also carried a knife, and his cane contained a sword.

Yancy's sidekick, Pahoo-Ka-Ta-Wah, used a sawed-off double-barrel shotgun, along with a knife. He never spoke, and the two communicated with sign language.

Mahoney came to the program after the series, *Range Rider*, and a series of films. He went on to play Tarzan in motion pictures.

Mahoney died in 1989 at the age of 70, X. Brands in 2000 at age 72.

Young Maverick

1979 – 1980 CBS, 8 episodes all one hour in color.

Cast:

Charles Frank as Ben Maverick
Susan Blanchard as Nell McGarrahan
John Dehner as Marshal Edge Troy

This series, developed by Juanita Bartlett, was a sequel to *Maverick*.
The pilot was the 1978 television movie, *The New Maverick*, which introduced Charles Frank as Ben, and featured original *Maverick* stars James Garner and Jack Kelly.
The theme song for this show was composed by David Buttolph.

Synopsis:

Two decades after *Maverick*, CBS failed to score ratings success with this sequel.
Maverick star James Garner appeared briefly in the opening scene of the first episode, as Bret ran into his younger cousin Ben, played by Frank.
Other regulars were the lovely, slick Nell, and the straight Marshal Troy, played by John Dehner, who died at age 76 in 1992.

Zorro

1957 – 1959 ABC, 78 thirty-minute black & white episodes; 1960-1961 ABC, four color "specials" each sixty minutes in length.

Cast:

Guy Williams as Don Diego de la Vega/Zorro
Gene Sheldon as Bernardo
George J. Lewis as Don Alejandro de la Vega

Zorro was created by Johnson McCully, who wrote more than sixty stories featuring the character. The theme song was composed by Norman Foster and George Bruns. The song was performed by both The Mellomen and The Chordettes.

Synopsis:

Zorro – the fox in Spanish – had two successful seasons before a dispute in ownership ceased production. After a one-year hiatus, the show was briefly revived in the form of four specials, in color and one hour long.

Played with dash by Guy Williams, *Zorro* was set in Spanish California. The character's name was Don Diego de la Vega, who was an apparent weakling.

But when trouble started Don would hide, put on a black mask, cape, hat, get his sword, and ride to the rescue.

The only person to share Don's secret was the apparently mute family servant, Bernardo.

Swordplay highlighted the action in this series, with the usual result that "Zorro" would win and cut a *Z* in his defeated enemy's clothing. Many of the stories were also on a continued basis.

Zorro has had a long film history, from 1920's *The Mask of Zorro* to a movie of the same name in 1998, and *The Legend of Zorro* in 2005. Zorro was also featured in a Republic Pictures cliffhanger series.

Two compilations from the series were released theatrically. And an attempt at comedy resulted in 1983's *Zorro and Son*, which lasted five episodes and starred Henry Darrow with Paul Regenia as the son.

Williams died at age 65 in 1989, Sheldon age 74 in 1982, Lewis age 91 in 1995.

###

Reflections, Facts, & Opinions

Following its success in the 1950s and early 1960s, television Westerns started to wane. The trend continued into the 1970s with the demise of *Bonanza* and *Gunsmoke*. A few new shows came and went.

It wasn't until the late 1980s, led by the magnificent mini-series *Lonesome Dove*, that a minor revival occurred. There were *Lonesome Dove* prequels, sequels, and a series. Several Western television films were produced, as were the previously mentioned *Gunsmoke* and *Bonanza* movies.

Kenny Rogers rode his massive hit song "The Gambler" through two television films and three mini-series. As has been noted throughout this book, the third production afforded a herd of Western television veterans to reprise their roles.

Weekly series – none of which lasted more than three years – included *Bordertown*, *The Young Riders*, *The Adventures of Briscoe County, Jr.*, and *Paradise* (which became *Guns of Paradise*).

Following in *The Gambler's* tracks, *Paradise* allowed a handful of Western veterans to ride once more. The 1988 CBS remake of *Red River*, featuring James Arness, did the same.

Two decades later, a noteworthy series was AMC's *Hell on Wheels*, which ended in 2016 after a run of five seasons and 57 episodes.

Five longest-running network shows

20 years – *Gunsmoke*, CBS
14 years – *Bonanza*, NBC
9 years – *The Virginian* NBC
8 years – *Cheyenne*, ABC & *Wagon Train* NBC & ABC (The syndicated *Death Valley Days* also aired 20 seasons.)

Five shows with the most episodes

635 – *Gunsmoke*

532 – *Death Valley Days*
428 – *Bonanza*
253 – *Wagon Train*
248 – *The Virginian*

Five highest-rated shows in a season

43.1 *Gunsmoke* in 1958
40.3 *Gunsmoke* in 1960
39.6 *Gunsmoke* in 1959
37.3 *Gunsmoke* in 1961
36.9 *Bonanza* in 1964 – Although this is the highest rating *Bonanza* recorded, the show finished second this season behind *The Beverly Hillbillies* and its 39.1.

Westerns ranked in the top twenty-five

Rating & Program
1st   *Gunsmoke* 1958, 1959, 1960, 1961
        Wagon Train 1962
        Bonanza 1965, 1966, 1967
2nd   *Wagon Train* 1959, 1960, 1961
        Bonanza 1962, 1964
        Gunsmoke 1970
3rd   *Tales of Wells Fargo* 1958
        Have Gun Will Travel 1959, 1960, 1961
        Gunsmoke 1962
        Bonanza 1969, 1970
4th   *Have Gun Will Travel* 1958
        The Rifleman 1959
        Bonanza 1963
        Gunsmoke & *Bonanza* (tie) 1968
        Gunsmoke 1972
5th   *Gunsmoke* 1971
6th   *The Life and Legend of Wyatt Earp* 1958
        Maverick 1959
        Rawhide 1961
        Gunsmoke 1969
7th   *The Lone Ranger* 1951
        Gunsmoke 1957, 1973
        Tales of Wells Fargo 1959
8th   *The Restless Gun* 1958
9th   *Hopalong Cassidy* 1951
        Wanted: Dead or Alive 1960
        Bonanza 1971

10th	*The Life and Legend of Wyatt Earp* 1959
	Gunsmoke 1963, *The Virginian* 1967
11th	(None)
12th	*Cheyenne* 1958
13th	*Dick Powell's Zane Grey Theater* 1959
	The Rifleman 1960
	Rawhide 1962
14th	*Branded* 1965
	The Virginian 1968
15th	*The Texan* 1959
	Lawman 1960
	Gunsmoke 1974
16th	*Wanted: Dead or Alive* 1959
	Lawman 1960
17th	*Cheyenne* 1960
	Bonanza 1961
	The Virginian 1964
	The Virginian 1969
18th	*The Lone Ranger* 1952
	The Life and Legend of Wyatt Earp 1957
	Cheyenne 1959
	Rawhide 1960
19th	*Maverick* 1960
20th	*The Life and Legend of Wyatt Earp* 1960
	Gunsmoke 1964
	Bonanza 1972
21st	*Dick Powell's Zane Grey Theater* 1958
	Sugarfoot 1959
	Dick Powell's Zane Grey Theater 1960
22nd	*Rawhide* 1963
	The Virginian 1965
23rd	*The Adventures of Rin Tin Tin* 1955
	Sugarfoot & *Wagon Train* (tie) 1958
	The Virginian & *The Wild, Wild West* (tie)
24th	(None)
25th	*Wagon Train* 1963

~~~

The apex of television Westerns was the 1958 – '59 season. Thirty-one Westerns aired, with seven in the top ten and 12 in the top 25. The previous season, nine had reached the top 25.

The following season, 1959 – '60, the top 25 contained 11 Westerns. The figure fell to five the next year, then four.

The 1960s ended with only two Westerns in the top 25.

~~~

(The following categories are subjective.)

Five lawmen you wouldn't want to face in a gunfight

Deputy J.D. Smith, played by Jack Elam, *The Dakotas*. A left eye which practiced free will had no effect on his swift draw.

Deputy Johnny McKay, played by Peter Brown, *Lawman*. The advantage of youth!

Marshal Matt Dillon, played by James Arness, *Gunsmoke*. Fast, accurate, fearless.

Special Agent Jim Hardie, played by Dale Robertson, *Tales of Wells Fargo*. This southpaw was fast and on target.

Ranger Clint Travis, played by Kelo Henderson in *26 Men*. A true-life gun artist who needed no Hollywood training.

Five citizens you wouldn't want to face in a gunfight

Bill Longley, played by Rory Calhoun, *The Texan*. Calhoun duplicated the real-life gunman who was noted for his speed with a gun.

Jess Harper, played by Robert Fuller, *Laramie*. An actor born for the television West.

Joe Cartwright, played by Michael Landon, *Bonanza*. A lefty who was smooth and quick.

Lucas McCain, played by Chuck Connors. *The Rifleman* standing tall, deadly rifle pointed and ready, was intimidation at its best.

Paladin, played by Richard Boone, *Have Gun Will Travel*, was a bounty hunter with lethal speed.

Five fellows you wouldn't want to get into a brawl with

Cheyenne Bodie, played by Clint Walker, *Cheyenne*. Broad-shouldered, a rock solid six and a half feet.

Dave Blassingame, played by Brian Keith, *The Westerner*. Solid as granite who didn't know the meaning of giving up.

Hoss Cartwright, played by Dan Blocker, *Bonanza*. When Hoss let loose – as he sometimes did in the early seasons of the show – no one was left standing.

Matt Dillon, played by James Arness, *Gunsmoke*. Six feet seven inches of toughness and grit.

Paladin, played by Richard Boone, *Have Gun, Will Travel*. In addition to his gunfighting skills, Paladin was a swordsman, a boxer, and had training in the martial arts.

Five fellows to ride the river with

Ben Cartwright, played by Lorne Greene, *Bonanza*. He carved his thousand square mile Ponderosa out of the Sierra Nevada mountains, buried three wives, had three sons, and adopted a fourth.

Gil Favor, played by Eric Fleming, *Rawhide*. This trail boss would get you there, one way or the other.

John Cannon, played by Leif Erickson, *The High Chaparral*. Big John made his mark by building a ranch in southern Arizona, while dealing with Mexicans, Apaches, outlaws, and land grabbers.

Matt Dillon, played by James Arness, *Gunsmoke*. The word "quit" was not in this lawman's vocabulary; trailing an owl hoot from Dodge City into Mexico was all in a week's work.

Sam Buckhart, played by Michael Ansara, *Law of the Plainsman*. An Apache who had the fortitude to be a United States Marshal.

Five made-for television guns

Johnny Ringo – His LeMat pistol was unique for the television West, even if it was an actual gun.

Shotgun Slade – A combination shotgun and rifle.

The Life and Legend of Wyatt Earp – A long-barreled pistol termed the Buntline Special did exist in the real West. Whether or not Earp actually used the gun is open to debate.

The Rifleman – The large loop lever was borrowed from John Wayne, but the set screw in the trigger guard was original.

Wanted: Dead or Alive – Instead of a sawed-off shotgun, a sawed-off rifle with a loop lever, which later became more of a triangle.

Five exceptional programs which deserved more than one season

The Dakotas – An excellent program which wasn't allowed to finish out the season.

The Loner – Rod Serling's atypical entry in the television West.

The Outcasts – An ex-slave and an ex-slave owner join forces as bounty hunters.

The Westerner – A drifter and his dog, meeting trouble at every turn.

Whiplash – A stage line vs. the Australian Aborigines.

Five memorable episodes not titled *Gunsmoke* or *Bonanza*

The Dakotas – "Sanctuary at Crystal Springs," written by Cy Chermak and directed by Richard Sarafian. Two killers rush into a church full of funeral mourners. Deputies Smith and Stark charge in after them. The ensuing brutal shootout, in which the outlaws are shot to pieces and the pastor is wounded, caused so much fan protest that the show was cancelled. Incredibly violent and intense, this episode also features a healthy dose of spirituality.

The Life and Legend of Wyatt Earp – "Gunfight at the O.K. Corral," written by Frederick Brennan, directed by Paul Landres. Arguably the single best-known event in the Old West, admirably depicted on the small screen.

The Rifleman – "Strange Town," written by Jack Lewis and directed by Joseph Lewis. McCain puts on a badge and goes after the man who beat Micah with a rock, and hung him on a barbed wire fence.

The Virginian – "The Showdown," written by Gene Coon and directed by Don McDougall. The Virginian, Michael Ansara as the marshal, and Leonard Nimoy as his deputy brother in a shootout with a gang of thieves.

The Westerner – "Jeff," written by Sam Peckinpah and Robert Heverly, directed by Sam Peckinpah. Dave Blassingame sets out after a young woman named Jeff. He has known Jeff since she was a child, and she is now a prostitute. In vintage Peckinpah, Blassingame gets into a shooting, a vicious fistfight, and twice meets a woman proclaiming the Word of God.

Single best night of Television Westerns

Saturday, 1959:
7:30 *Bonanza* NBC
8:30 *Wanted Dead or Alive* CBS
9:00 *The Deputy* NBC
9:30 *Have Gun Will Travel* CBS
10:00 *Gunsmoke* CBS

Images of a Golden Time

William Boyd, top left, starred as *Hopalong Cassidy*. His nemesis is not known. Lower photo, Dale Robertson was Ben Calhoun in *Iron Horse*. He earlier played Jim Hardie for five seasons in *Tales of Wells Fargo*.

Some of *Bonanza's* most memorable episodes featured Hoss – portrayed by Dan Blocker – in a comedy. He was determined to win the $500 prize of "The Flapjack Contest," in spite of a bank robbery taking place.

The Wild Wild West co-starred Robert Conrad, right, as James T. West. One of the more notable villains on the show was Dr. Miguelito Loveless, played by Michael Dunn.

Robert Fuller co-starred in both *Laramie* and *Wagon Train*, and made guest appearances in dozens of other shows.

Robert Horton, left, and Ward Bond co-starred the first four seasons of *Wagon Train*. Bond played Major Seth Adams, the wagon master, and Horton was his scout, Flint McCullough. Bond passed away after the fourth season, and McCullough left after the fifth. The show lasted eight years.

Lloyd Bridges was *The Loner*, an unconventional Western created by Rod Sterling. He played Civil War veteran William Colton.

Gene Autry was the first Western movie star to appear in a regular television series. His *Gene Autry Show* ran for six seasons.

Above, some of the Warner Brothers stable of Western stars, from left, Will Hutchins of *Sugarfoot*, Peter Brown of *Lawman*, Jack Kelly of *Maverick*, Ty Hardin of *Bronco*, James Garner of *Maverick*, Wayde Preston of *Colt .45*, John Russell of *Lawman*. Left, Steve McQueen as bounty hunter Josh Randall in *Wanted Dead or Alive*.

"Hoss and the Leprechauns" is arguably *Bonanza's* best-loved comedy episode. The "little green men" were played by Frank Delfino, Harry Monte, Felix Silla, Nels Nelson, and Roger Arroya. The Cartwrights were, left, Dan Blocker as Hoss and Pernell Roberts as Adam; right, Michael Landon as Little Joe and Lorne Greene as Ben.

The Life and Legend of Wyatt Earp featured Hugh O'Brian as the marshal, with his Buntline Special pistol. The show followed a specific time frame in Earp's life, concluding with the gunfight at the O.K. Corral.

Roy Rogers, the "King of the Cowboys," starred in *The Roy Rogers Show*. Rogers had his horse, Trigger, stuffed and mounted when the animal died.

James Arness, right, as Marshal Matt Dillon and Dennis Weaver as Chester Goode in the 1958 *Gunsmoke* episode, "The Patsy." The program was television's quintessential Western.

Two excellent Westerns at the opposite ends of longevity. *The Dakotas*, top, aired 19 episodes, *Gunsmoke* 635. The cast of *The Dakotas*, from left, Mike Greene, Larry Ward, Jack Elam, Chad Everett. The veteran *Gunsmoke* cast, seated, Buck Taylor; standing, from left, Ken Curtis, Milburn Stone, Amanda Blake, James Arness, Glenn Strange.

The *Bonanza* cast for its first six seasons: Lorne Greene, seated; standing from left, Dan Blocker, Michael Landon, Pernell Roberts. They portrayed Ben, Hoss, Little Joe, and Adam Cartwright.

For six seasons, Clint Eastwood, left, and Eric Fleming co-starred on *Rawhide* as ramrod Rowdy Yates and trail boss Gil Favor. After Fleming departed, Eastwood's Yates took over the drive. The show was cancelled mid-way through season seven.

James Arness as Matt Dillon, *Gunsmoke*. Arness played the character from the show's premier in 1955 until the last television movie in 1994.

David Carradine walked the West as Kwai Chang Caine for three years on *Kung Fu*. He returned for two television movie sequels. Carradine won the part over Bruce Lee.

David Soul co-starred on *Here Comes the Brides* for two seasons. The theme song, "Seattle," was a hit for Perry Como. Soul later co-starred in *Starsky and Hutch*.

Images of a Golden Time ◆ **137**

F Troop enjoyed two seasons of comedy. Primary cast members were, from left, a mounted Forrest Tucker, Larry Storch, Melody Patterson, and Ken Berry.

Two of the three longest-running network Westerns were *Gunsmoke* and *The Virginian*. James Drury, top, was referred to only as *The Virginian*. James Arness was *Gunsmoke's* Marshal Matt Dillon.

Guy Williams had the lead role in the popular *Zorro*. Legal difficulties limited production to two seasons, and four one-hour specials.

The Adventures of Rin Tin Tin was popular enough to last five seasons. The human stars were Lee Aaker, left, and James Brown. The identity of the individual on the right is not known.

Johnny Crawford played Mark McCain five seasons on *The Rifleman*. In 1959, Crawford received an Emmy nomination for Best Supporting Actor in a Dramatic Series.

Lawman featured four seasons of well-produced, straight-shooting episodes. Laramie Marshal Dan Troop was portrayed by John Russell, left. Peter Brown was his deputy, Johnny McKay.

Matt and Kitty. For fans of Western television, no further explanation is needed. Amanda Blake played Miss Kitty Russell for 19 seasons of *Gunsmoke* and the first television movie. James Arness, as Marshall Matt Dillon, is a television icon.

Michael Landon as Joe Cartwright, *Bonanza*. During the course of the show, Landon expanded his abilities to include both writing, and directing.

Milburn Stone, left, won an Emmy for his performance in the *Gunsmoke* episode, "Baker's Dozen," as he attempts to find a home for orphaned triplets. Festus (Ken Curtis) tries to help.

Clint Walker was *Cheyenne* for eight seasons. The character was a former scout who roamed the West after the Civil War.

Chuck Connors as Lucas McCain, *The Rifleman*. The widower was a rancher raising his son Mark and helping North Fork, New Mexico Marshal Micah Torrance. Note the set screw in the trigger guard.

Clayton Moore, left, was the actor most identified as *The Lone Ranger*. Jay Silverheels was his sidekick, Tonto.

Pernell Roberts portrayed oldest son Adam Cartwright on the first six seasons of *Bonanza*. After Roberts left, the character continued to be mentioned for several seasons.

References

Information for this book was gleaned...

From viewing numerous episodes of the various series, from watching and listening to television and radio interviews with producers, directors, and actors, from perusing various web sites, and from the following publications:

A History of Television's The Virginian, 1962-1971, by Paul Green.

Back in the Saddle – Essays on Western Film and Television Actors, by Gary A. Yoggy.

Bonanza – A Viewer's Guide to the TV Legend, by David R. Greenland.

Classic TV Westerns – A Pictorial History, by Ronald Jackson.

First Official TV Western Book, by Neil Summers.

Gunsmoke – A Complete History, by SuzAnne Barabas and Gabor Barabas.

Gunsmoke – An American Institution, by Ben Costello.

James Arness – An Autobiography, by James Arness with James W. Wise Jr.

Louisville Courier-Journal.

Louisville Times.

The Complete Directory to Prime-Time Network and Cable TV Shows, by Tim Brooks and Earle Marsh.

Rawhide – A History of Television's Longest Cattle Drive, by David R. Greenland.

Riding the Video Range – The Rise and Fall of the Western on Television, by Gary A. Yoggy.

Saturday Evening Post.

The Gunsmoke Chronicles – A New History of Television's Greatest Western, by David R. Greenland.

The Television Years, by Arthur Shulman and Roger Youman.
The TV Theme Song Sing-Along Book, by John Javna.
TV Guide.
TV Radio Mirror.
Western Clippings by Boyd Magers.
Who Shot the Sheriff? The Rise and Fall of the Television Western, by J. Fred MacDonald.
Wildest Westerns.

Index of shows

A Man Called Shenandoah: 48
Action in the Afternoon: 48, 49
Alias Smith & Jones: 49, 50
Annie Oakley: 50

Barbary Coast: 50, 51
Bat Masterson: 51
Bonanza: 1, 16-28, 44, 45, 52, 56, 91, 96, 97, 111-116, 119, 126, 127, 132, 144, 149, 150
Branded: 51, 52, 113
Brave Eagle: 52
Broken Arrow: 53, 73
Boots and Saddles: 53
Bronco: 30, 34, 54, 81, 125
Buckskin: 54
Buffalo Bill Jr.: 55

Casey Jones: 55
Cheyenne: 30, 31, 34, 54, 81, 88, 111, 113, 114, 146
Cimarron City: 56
Cimarron Strip: 56
Colt .45: 57, 125
Cowboy G-Men: 57, 58
Cowboys & Injuns: 58
Cowboy Theater: 58
Custer: 58, 59

Death Valley Days: 31, 62, 111, 112
Destry: 59

Dick Powell's Zane Grey Theater: 31, 32, 42, 63, 69, 101, 103, 113
Dirty Sally: 60
Dundee & the Culhane: 60
Dusty's Trail: 61

F Troop: 61, 62, 85, 137
Frontier: 62
Frontier Circus: 62, 63
Frontier Doctor: 63
Frontier Justice: 63

Gunslinger: 64
Gunsmoke: 1, 3-15, 17, 22, 26, 31, 35, 42, 44, 45, 60, 67, 111-116, 130, 131, 134, 138, 143, 145, 150

Have Gun Will Travel: 5, 32, 33, 112, 114, 115, 116
Here Comes the Brides: 64, 65, 136
Hondo: 65
Hopalong Cassidy: 65, 66, 112, 118
Hotel de Pardee: 66
How the West Was Won: 12, 67

Iron Horse: 67, 68

Jefferson Drum: 68
Johnny Ringo: 32, 68, 69, 115

Kung Fu: 69, 70, 78, 135

Index of shows ♦ 153

Lancer: 70
Laramie: 46, 56, 71, 114, 121
Laredo: 71, 72
Lash of the West: 72
Law of the Plainsman: 72, 73, 115
Lawman: 34, 72, 73, 74, 113, 114, 125, 142

MacKenzie's Raiders: 74
Man from Blackhawk: 74
Man Without a Gun: 75
Maverick: 33, 34, 35, 49, 109, 112, 113, 125

Overland Trail: 75

Pony Express: 76

Range Rider: 76, 108
Rango: 76, 77
Rawhide: 5, 34, 35, 70, 112, 113, 115, 133, 150

Sara: 77
Saturday Roundup: 78
Shane: 78
Shotgun Slade: 78, 79, 115
Stagecoach West: 79
Steve Donovan, Western Marshal: 80
Stories of the Century: 80
Sugarfoot: 30, 34, 54, 81, 113, 125

Tales of the Texas Rangers: 81, 82
Tales of Wells Fargo: 35, 36, 68, 112, 114, 118
Temple Houston: 82
Tate: 82, 83
Texas John Slaughter: 83
The Adventures of Champion: 83, 84
The Adventures of Judge Roy Bean: 84
The Adventures of Kit Carson: 84, 85
The Adventures of Rin Tin Tin: 36, 37, 113, 140
The Alaskans: 85
The Big Valley: 85, 86
The Black Saddle: 86, 87

The Californians: 87
The Chisholms: 88
The Cisco Kid: 37
The Dakotas: 88, 89, 114, 115, 116, 131
The Deputy: 89, 116
The Gabby Hayes Show: 90
The Gene Autry Show: 38, 124
The Guns of Will Sonnett: 90, 91
The High Chaparral: 91, 92, 115
The Legend of Jessie James: 92
The Life and Legend of Wyatt Earp: 38, 39, 112, 113, 115, 116, 128
The Lone Ranger: 37, 39-41, 76, 112, 113, 148
The Loner: 92, 93, 115, 123
The Marshal of Gunsight Pass: 93
The Monroes: 93, 94
The Nine Lives of Elfego Baca: 94
The Outcasts: 94, 95, 115
The Outlaws: 95
The Quest: 95, 96
The Rebel: 96
The Restless Gun: 17, 96, 97, 112
The Rifleman: 32, 41, 42, 52, 71, 73, 112-116, 141, 147
The Road West: 97
The Rough Riders: 97, 98
The Rounders: 98
The Roy Rogers Show: 43, 129
The Tall Man: 98, 99
The Texan: 99, 113, 114
The Travels of Jaimie McPheeters: 99, 100
The Virginian: 43-45, 51, 56, 72, 75, 111, 112, 113, 116, 138, 150
The Westerner: 32, 100, 101, 114-116
The Wild Wild West: 51, 101, 120
Tombstone Territory: 102
Trackdown: 32, 102, 103
26 Men: 103, 114
Two Faces West: 104

Union Pacific: 104

Wagon Train: 30, 35, 45, 46, 48, 71, 111-113, 121, 122
Wanted Dead or Alive: 103, 105, 116, 125

Whiplash: 105, 106, 115
Whispering Smith: 106
Wichita Town: 107
Wild Bill Hickok: 107
Wrangler: 108

Yancy Derringer: 108
Young Maverick: 109

Zorro: 21, 107, 109, 110, 139

Index of actors

Aaker, Lee: 36, 37, 140
Adams, Nick: 96
Ahn, Phillip: 69, 70
Allen, Rex: 63
Anderson, John: 39
Anderson, Michael Jr.: 93
Andrews, Stanley: 31
Ansara, Michael: 41, 53, 73, 115, 116
Arness, James: 3-12, 67, 111, 114, 115, 130, 131, 134, 138, 143, 150
Autry, Gene: 38, 84, 124
Ayres, Lew: 63

Bardette, Trevor: 39
Barry, Gene: 51
Bateman, Charles: 104
Baur, Elizabeth: 70
Bell, Rex: 58
Bellamy, Ralph: 63
Bendix, William: 75
Berry, Ken: 61, 62, 137
Bickford, Charles: 44
Blake, Amanda: 3, 4, 7-10, 131, 143
Blair, Patricia: 41
Blanchard, Susan: 109
Blocker, Dan: 16, 18-20, 22-24, 26, 56, 114, 119, 126, 132
Blondell, Joan: 64, 65
Bond, Ward: 45, 46, 122
Boone, Randy: 44
Boone, Richard: 5, 32, 33, 114, 115
Boxleitner, Bruce: 12, 67
Boyd, William: 65, 66, 118

Brand, Neville: 50, 71, 72
Brands, X.: 108
Brady, Pat: 43
Brady, Scott: 79
Bray, Robert: 79
Breck, Peter: 85-87
Brennan, Walter: 50, 90, 91
Bridges, Lloyd: 92, 93, 123
Briles, Charles: 86
Brinegar, Paul: 34, 35, 38, 70
Bronson, Charles: 99, 100
Brophy, Sallie: 54
Brown, James: 36, 37, 140
Brown, Peter: 34, 71-74, 114, 125, 142
Brown, Robert: 64
Buchanan, Edgar: 65, 66, 84
Buttram, Pat: 38

Calhoun, Rory: 99, 114
Canary, David: 16, 21, 24, 27
Carey, Philip: 71, 72
Carlson, Richard: 74
Carradine, David: 69, 70, 78, 135
Carrillo, Leo: 37
Case, Allen: 89, 92
Cassell, Barry: 48
Castle, Mary: 80
Castle, Peggy: 73, 74
Clark, Bobby: 55
Clarke, Gary: 44
Cobb, Lee J.: 43-45
Coffin, Tris: 103
Collier, Don: 95

Connors, Chuck: 41, 42, 51, 52, 114, 147
Conrad, Robert: 101, 120
Conway, Pat: 102
Conway, Tim: 76, 77
Coogan, Jackie: 57, 58
Corcoran, Kelly: 97
Corrigan, Lloyd: 38
Coy, Walter: 62
Crawford, Bobby Jr.: 71
Crawford, Johnny: 41, 42, 71, 141
Cristal, Linda: 91
Cullen, William K.: 67
Culp, Robert: 102, 103
Cummings, Susan: 104
Curtis, Barry: 83
Curtis, Ken: 3, 4, 6, 7, 9, 131, 145

Darrow, Henry: 91, 110
Davis, Gail: 50
Davis, Jim: 80
Davis, Roger: 49, 50
Dean, Eddie: 93
Dehner, John: 44, 100, 109
Denver, Bob: 61
Derek, John: 62, 63
Devine, Andy: 107
Diamond, Don: 84, 85
Dorell, Don: 76
Douglas, Melvyn: 63
Drury, James: 43-45, 50, 138
Duel, Pete: 49, 50
Duggan, Andrew: 70
Durant, Don: 68

Eastham, Richard: 102
Eastwood, Clint: 34, 35, 133
Elam, Jack: 25, 50, 82, 88, 89, 114, 131
Erickson, Leif: 91, 92, 115
Evans, Dale: 43
Evans, Linda: 85, 86
Everett, Chad: 88, 89, 131
Evers, Jason: 90, 91, 108
Ewing, Roger: 3, 9

Fix, Paul: 41, 42, 50
Flanagan, Fionnula: 67
Fleming, Eric: 34, 35, 115, 133

Fonda, Henry: 89
Fowley, Douglas: 38
Frank, Charles: 109
Fuller, Robert: 24, 45, 46, 71, 114, 121

Garner, James: 33, 34, 109, 125
Garrison, Sean: 60
Gaynor, Jock: 95
Gulager, Clu: 44, 98, 99
Goddard, Mark: 69
Granger, Stewart: 44
Graves, Peter: 105, 106
Greene, Lorne: 16, 17, 19, 21, 22, 24-26, 115, 126, 127, 132
Greene, Mike: 88, 89, 131

Hale, Alan Jr.: 55
Hall, Monty: 58
Hardin, Ty: 34, 54, 125
Harris, Rosemary: 88
Hart, John: 40
Hawkins, Jimmy: 50
Hayden, Russell: 57, 58, 93
Hayes, Gabby: 90
Hayes, Ron: 98
Henderson, Kelo: 103, 114
Hershey, Barbara: 93
Holliman, Earl: 66
Horton, Robert: 45, 46, 48, 122
Hunter, Jeffrey: 82
Hutchins, Will: 34, 81, 125

Ireland, Jill: 78

Jaeckel, Richard: 62, 63
Jones, Christopher: 92
Jones, Dick: 55, 76
Jones, L.Q.: 30
Johnson, Brad: 50
Johnson, Russell: 86, 87
Jordan, Ted: 9

Keith, Brian: 100, 101, 114
Kelly, Jack: 33, 34, 109, 125
Kennedy, Adam: 87
Kennedy, Douglas: 80
Kramer, Burt: 77

Index of actors ♦ 157

Landon, Michael: 16, 18, 20-24, 26-28, 114, 126, 127, 132, 144
Larsen, Keith: 52
LaRue, Lash: 72
Lauter, Harry: 81, 82
Leonard, Mark: 64, 65
Lewis, George J.: 109, 110
Lewis, Judy: 95
Locke, Tammy: 94
Loggia, Robert: 94
London, Dirk: 38
Long, Richard: 85, 86
Lu, Lisa: 32
Luke, Keye: 69, 70
Lupton, John: 53

MacLane, Barton: 95
Madison, Guy: 107
Mahoney, Jock: 76, 108
Majors, Lee: 50, 85, 86
Marks, Guy: 76, 77
Martin, Eugene: 68
Martin, Ross: 101
Matheson, Tim: 21, 95, 96
Maunder, Wayne: 59, 70
May, Donald: 57
Maynard, Kermit: 78
McClory, Sean: 87
McClure, Doug: 43-45, 50, 51, 75
McCrea, Jody: 107
McCrea, Joel: 44, 107
McGrath, Frank: 45, 46
McIntire, John: 44-46
McLean, David: 83
McQueen, Steve: 105, 125
Merlin, Jan: 97, 98
Milford, John: 92
Miller, Kristine: 80
Mills, John: 60
Mills, Mort: 75
Mitchell, Cameron: 91, 92
Montgomery, George: 56
Moore, Clayton: 40, 41, 148
Moore, Roger: 33, 34, 85
Morrow, Jeff: 104
Murdock, James: 34, 35
Murphy, Audie: 106

Murphy, Ben: 49, 88
Murray, Don: 94

Nolan, Jeanette: 60
Nolan, Tommy: 54
Nomkeena, Keena: 52
Nusser, James: 9

O'Brian, Hugh: 35, 38, 39, 128
O'Herlihy, Dan: 99, 100
Osmond Brothers: 100

Parker, Willard: 81, 82
Payne, John: 96, 97
Pera, Radames: 69
Pickens, Slim: 59, 95
Powell, Dick: 31, 32, 42, 63, 69, 101, 103, 113
Pratt, Judd: 104
Preston, Robert: 88
Preston, Wayde: 57, 125
Prine, Andrew: 97

Rambo, Dack: 60, 90
Reason, Rex: 75
Reynolds, Burt: 3, 7, 9
Richards, Jeff: 68
Ritter, Blake: 48
Road, Michael: 54
Roberts, Pernell: 16, 17, 19-21, 24, 26, 27, 50, 126, 132, 149
Robertson, Dale: 31, 35, 36, 67, 68, 114, 118
Rockwell, Robert: 74
Rogers, Roy: 43, 129
Rogers, Wayne: 79
Reagan, Ronald: 31
Renaldo, Duncan: 37
Russell, Bing: 16, 21
Russell, John: 34, 50, 73, 74, 125, 142
Russell, Kurt: 95, 96, 99, 100

Schultz, Keith: 94
Schultz, Kevin: 94
Scott, Brenda: 97
Scott, Pippa: 44
Sen Yung, Victor: 16, 21

Sharpe, Karen: 68
Shatner, William: 50, 51
Sheldon, Gene: 109, 110
Sherman, Bobby: 64, 65
Shore, Roberta: 43, 44
Silvera, Frank: 91, 92
Silverheels, Jay: 40, 41, 148
Slade, Mark: 91
Smith, Hal: 68
Smith, John: 56, 71
Smith, William: 71, 72
Soul, David: 64, 65, 136
Stacy, James: 70
Stanwyck, Barbara: 85, 86
Stevenson, Robert: 68
Stone, Milburn: 3, 4, 7, 9, 11, 13, 131, 145
Strange, Glenn: 3, 9, 131
Sullivan, Barry: 97-99
Sullivan, Grant: 76

Taeger, Ralph: 65
Taylor, Buck: 3, 8-10, 131
Taylor, Dub: 55
Taylor, Joan: 41
Taylor, Kent: 97, 98
Taylor, Robert: 31
Teal, Ray: 16, 21
Tong, Kam: 32

Totter, Audrey: 56
Tryon, Tom: 83
Tucker, Forrest: 61, 62, 137

Vaccaro, Brenda: 77
Valentine, Jack: 48, 49
Vogel, Mitch: 16, 22, 24

Waller, Eddy: 80
Watts, Mary: 48
Walker, Clint: 30, 31, 34, 81, 114, 146
Ward, Larry: 88, 89, 131
Wayne, Patrick: 98
Weaver, Dennis: 3, 4, 6, 7, 9, 42, 44, 130
Whitman, Stuart: 56
Whitney, Peter: 97, 98
Wilkes, Robert: 92
Williams, Bill: 84, 85
Williams, Guy: 21, 109, 110, 139
Wills, Chill: 62, 63, 98
Wilson, Terry: 45, 46
Winono, Kim: 52
Wolders, Robert: 71, 72
Woodward, Morgan: 11, 39
Wooley, Sheb: 34, 35

Yarnall, Bruce: 95
York, Jeff: 85
Young, Otis: 94, 95

About the author

Lanny Tucker is a life-long fan of television Westerns. He was previously employed in the newspaper field, where he won numerous awards from the Kentucky Press Association for writing and photography.

He has written two books of historical fiction. *Deeds of Blood 1840* was inspired by events which occurred in central Kentucky. *Micajah Harpe, Vampire* features the country's first known serial killer – who was decapitated in 1799 – returning from the dead during the Civil War.

He has also published four books pertaining to his place of residence.

History of Green County, Kentucky chronicles the development and significant events of his home county. *Osceola, the Lost River Town of Green County* tells of the town which was lost to the flood waters of Little Barren River.

Historical Photos of Green County, Kentucky, features over one hundred photographs, several more than a century old, of historical interest.

And his book of landscape photography, *Photos in Green*, depicts current scenes of Green County, Kentucky.

The End

www.ingramcontent.com/pod-product-compliance
Lightning Source LLC
Chambersburg PA
CBHW051105160426
43193CB00010B/1326